Torment and Tequila in Belle Epoque Mexico

José López Portillo y Rojas (1850–1923), 1914; Library of Congress, Prints and Photographs Division, reproduction number LC-DIG-ggbain-15739

Torment and Tequila in Belle Epoque Mexico

Four Short Works of Fiction by José López Portillo y Rojas

Translated and Edited by Terry Rugeley

The University of Alabama Press
Tuscaloosa

The University of Alabama Press
Tuscaloosa, Alabama 35487–0380
uapress.ua.edu

Typeface: Janson Text LT Std

Cover image: Perpendicular cliffs of the Santiago River Canyon, Guadalajara, Mexico, 1919; photograph courtesy of the Library of Congress
Cover design: Sandy Turner Jr.

Cataloging-in-Publication data is available from the Library of Congress.
ISBN: 978-0-8173-6235-5 (paper)
E-ISBN: 978-0-8173-9584-1

Contents

Acknowledgments

THIS VOLUME HAS ONLY MADE it to the public owing to the contributions of some thoughtful, dedicated individuals, and to them I am especially grateful. Special thanks to Wendi Schnaufer of the University of Alabama Press for her unwavering faith in a collection of José López Portillo y Rojas's fiction. Two anonymous readers provided valuable suggestions for improving the manuscript. I would also like to extend a tip of the historical hat to Gary Moreno for bringing me up to speed on the *charro* culture of western Mexico. Finally, thanks to Margarita for listening to blow-by-blow accounts from an eccentric translator and for her many clarifications of things Mexican.

Introduction: A Patrician and His Prose

Whoever studies the genealogies of Mexican power must be struck by that power's ability to endure. Prominent people often come from prominent ancestors, illustrious last names retain their shine, money stays put, parents groom children for leadership, and family links to Spanish settlers and noblemen form a physical and mental double helix.

Few cases better illustrate the point than that of José López Portillo y Rojas (1850–1923), outstanding man of letters from that quintessentially western Mexican state of Jalisco. Few people read López Portillo today, and that is a shame. If we know of him at all, it is likely in connection with his grandson José López Portillo y Pacheco, president of Mexico from 1976 to 1982. (The two men bear a striking resemblance to each other, reminding us that money is not the only thing that gets handed down: take the late president, add round spectacles and handlebar mustache, fill out the nose a bit, and you have his grandfather.) Bitter controversy still surrounds those six years of the president's term, a time that began with the discovery of dazzling petroleum wealth but somehow ended in economic catastrophe, capital flight, banks nationalized to no good effect, and a humiliating peso devaluation: in brief, the flaming collapse of revolutionary dreams. The twelve years of neopopulism that were the presidencies of López Portillo and his friend and highly influential predecessor Luis Echeverría Álvarez (1970–76) stir up such conflicting memories that even today we lack a comprehensive study of their lives and times. But there is no need, and indeed no meaningful possibility, of somehow reading the López Portillo presidency backward onto the past. We have to see the grandfather not as grandfather, but rather as a figure of importance in his own time, an individual of both cultural and political engagement, and with a considerable corpus of literary production to his name. And there can be few better ways of entering his world than through his own writings.

This volume presents the modern reader with a brief anthology of López Portillo's prose corpus. The originals used for translation come from the four-volume *Obras del Lic. D. J. López Portillo y Rojas.*[1] López Portillo wrote a great deal, not all of which was suitable for this collection. I eliminated his nonfiction material, which includes his travel account of Europe and the Middle East and his biography of Mexican revolutionary leader Francisco Madero. Unsuitable as well were his full-length novels; indeed, *La parcela* alone is easily twice the size of the current volume, but we can enjoy a much briefer novella: *Nieves*, published serially in 1887, is probably his most frequently cited work today and still succeeds as both a literary creation and a window to the troubles of his age. To complement this better-known piece, I have also included three short stories that capture some of the author's main themes and fascinations: "El boleto de lotería" ("The Lottery Ticket"), "El espejo" ("The Mirror"), and "El brazalete" ("The Bracelet"). Two criteria determined their selection. First, López Portillo was a builder of national literature, and for that reason the stories needed to reference Mexican society in one way or another. His short story canon does include some works disembodied from time and place, and, although these are interesting enough, they were less germane to the present collection. Second, I looked for works that I thought embodied the themes discussed here: social frustration, loss, heartache, and the problems attending late-nineteenth-century development. López Portillo did have a taste for the supernatural; perhaps stories of ghosts and goblins were sellable, or perhaps he himself had caught the paranormal bug, a condition that like certain tropical diseases abates but never disappears entirely. It is hard to do anything new with well-plowed narratives like selling one's soul to the devil, so I rejected "Un pacto con el diablo" ("A Pact with the Devil") in favor of the far more personal "El espejo." Collectively, these four fictional stories give the modern reader some idea of why López Portillo was so widely admired in turn-of-the-century México and of the significant role he played in the construction of a national literature.

The Life and Times of José López Portillo y Rojas

The life and career of José López Portillo y Rojas conform to certain patterns common to nineteenth-century Mexico's literary set. Everything about López Portillo y Rojas established him as what the famous Uruguayan critic Ángel Rama called a *letrado*, one of those privileged intelligentsia who, by reason of literacy and learning, served as custodians of Latin America's symbolic world. Letrados asserted their influence early in the colonial period, survived the wars of independence, and spent the next two centuries fighting off challenges by populist forces. In Rama's telling, letrados moved to assume the role formerly occupied by churchmen and after 1870 became social theorists and even politicians in their own right. Yet these men were no subversives. Indeed, two important factors kept them loyal to Latin American *caudillo* leaders.[2] The letrados lacked a popular base and thus depended on the state for patronage. Moreover, they feared the masses, with their poverty, their resentment, and their scrambled ethnicity. Patrician scorn historically directed at enslaved and indigenous peoples found new targets as waves of immigrants began to enter Latin America after the mid-nineteenth century. It was no accident that the first Latin American academies of language and letters emerged at this time, because academies promised a *cordon sanitaire* against mass contamination of letrado culture. First came the Colombian academy in 1870, with Mexico forming its own five years later. But above all, letrados recognized the importance of the authoritarian modernizing state, with its laws and jails and constabulary, as the best means of containment. For those reasons, turn-of-the-century letrados tended to be ideological spear carriers, or at their most dangerous, friendly critics of the regimes they served.[3]

José López Portillo's education placed him among a single-digit percentage of the population of Jalisco, a rugged state known for horsemanship, sharpshooting, and old-school Spanish Catholicism. Small, independent ranchos coexisted with a few wealthy haciendas, many of them oriented toward the urban markets of the state's capital and main city, Guadalajara. Indeed, that city enjoyed such a brisk commercial life that its residents came to be known, then as now, as *Tapatíos*, from an old Nahuatl bartering term meaning "worth three." Some two hundred miles to the west lay the broad Pacific Ocean, accessible initially via the tiny port of San Blas. It was through here that many of the goods from the lucrative Manila trade, together with elements of the vast knowledge of the Orient, passed into Spain's hands. In the century's latter half, however, Puerto Vallarta, a more sheltered location and geographically closer to Jalisco's main city, assumed the role of leading port.

The López Portillo family's regional ascendency dated back to seventeenth-century settlements in the western province of Nueva Galicia, where Spanish presence centered around Guadalajara, later to become Mexico's second-largest city. But blood was not the only thing blue in López Portillo's veins. On his mother's side, the Rojas family had long-standing connections with the agave plant known as blue maguey and its distinctive distillate, tequila. And because this liquor plays such an essential role in the main story of this collection, it merits exploration. (By way of quick clarification, "mezcal" or "mescal" is a generic term for an agave distillate, whereas "tequila" refers specifically to liquor distilled from the *maguey azul*.[4])

Tequila's story began in 1758, when Spanish King Fernando VI gave José Antonio de Cuervo y Valdés royal permission to plant agaves in Nueva Galicia on his newly formed estate, La Cofradía de las Ánimas. In 1785 Fernando's successor, Carlos III, smelling economic independence in the colonies, prohibited liquor distillation in the Americas, but there is good reason to doubt the strength of this ban; after all, colonials were expert in ignoring or circumventing imperial decrees not to their liking. The prohibition ended in 1795, when Don Antonio's son, José María Guadalupe Cuervo y Marín y Montaño (b. 1708), received the right to distribute distilled liquor. Latin America's first commercial liquor company, named José Cuervo, was born.[5] His distillery-factory was also the first of its kind in Latin America. What we know as tequila was invented here; however, the original taste would have differed considerably from the over-the-counter descendant retailed today throughout the world, for many of the heirloom species the historic José Cuervo distilled no longer exist. Over time the property's name morphed into Taberna (or Teberna) de Cuervo, that is, "Cuervo's tavern," probably an indication that people were buying liquor by the drink there. But this second Don José passed away in the late 1700s, leaving the estate to his daughter María Magdalena Guadalupe Marín y Montaño.

Following the death of her first husband, in 1810 Doña María took the momentous step of marrying the enterprising José Vicente Albino Rosas (1790–1868). His dynamism and organizational skills made him the manager of the family estate, and the surname Rosas now took precedent over the original Cuervo. Don Vicente provided the model for the unnamed grandfather of *Nieves:* a man of action who strode through life as confidently as he strode through the agave fields. He was as comfortable in both office and the distillery, a larger-than-life patron of enterprise and patriarch of the family, a dynamo who revitalized the hacienda into the powerhouse of three million agave plants the novella describes, and who rechristened the distillery as La Rojeña, a name it retains today. He somehow managed to hold his own against political upheavals and the burning Jalisco sun in those difficult days before the coming of the railroad in 1888. When his first wife, María Magdalena, died, Don Vicente married María Rojas Flores de la Torre, grandmother of José López Portillo y Rojas. But while Don Vicente managed La Rojeña like a feudal lord, later ownership passed to his nephew Jesús Flores (via his first marriage), then on through a complicated line involving Flores's widow, Anita González Rubio, then her niece Virginia Gallardo González, and finally, via Virginia's marriage to German consul Juan Beckmann, to the Beckmann descendants, where it remains today.[6]

José López Portillo y Rojas therefore inherited a surname and some family wealth but not the actual hacienda or distillery. Growing up as a privileged child, he spent his entire life in the pursuit of the urban passions described presently. Moreover, textual evidence suggests that it was actually his cousins who were trying to keep the property going. *Nieves* probably grew from fictionalized memories of visits to the family estate, a world that apparently intrigued but also scandalized the educated young man of letters. And while it is tempting to link him to Aurelio López Paredes, founder of the factory Tequila de San José del Refugio, in Amatitán, Jalisco, we must recall that "López Portillo" was an *apellido compuesto*—that is, an inseparable combination of names, like "Ponce de León" or "Cabeza de Vaca"—and that there would have been no real etymological link between the two last names. Nor was the paternal last name of his second wife, Margarita Weber Narváez in any way connected with blue maguey's scientific designation *(Agave tequilana Weber)* named rather for the German naturalist Frédéric Albert Constantin Weber, who in the late nineteenth century spent many years constructing the taxonomy of Mexican flora and fauna. The actual scientific name of the plant was only coined in 1896, twelve years after José López Portillo married Margarita, in 1884. But despite all the changes of the twentieth century, the family tree retained pride in its agave roots. Indeed, in the last year of his life, ex-president José López Portillo y Pacheco had begun work on a novel entitled *La Rojeña,* a fictionalized account of the life of his great-great-grandfather Vicente Albino Rojas y Jiménez. This fact comes from López Portillo y Pacheco's grandson, who reports that work was underway as of five months before his grandfather's death in Mexico City in February 2004.[7] Family memories endured.

On his father's side, José López Portillo y Rojas hailed from a long line of creoles (pure-blooded Spaniards born in the Americas) whose progenitors had come west to participate in the Zacatecas mining boom of the late sixteenth century. Little is known about their colonial activities. Doubtless they struggled to establish themselves through mining, agriculture, and commerce, the only real economic activities that existed there. Creoles married creoles and begat still more creoles, but beyond that they did nothing to make them stand above the flow of history. His grandfather Pío Quinto López Portillo y Pacheco would have been present when independence leader Miguel Hidalgo's ragtag army occupied the city on November 26, 1810, and the radical priest issued a series of antipatrician decrees, such as the abolition of slavery. But the populist interregnum was brief. Don Pío must have sighed in relief when Hidalgo's forces crumbled in their last battle outside the city, at Puente de Calderón.

Moving to the post-independence period, we find the author's father, Jesús López Portillo, briefly serving as governor of the state of Jalisco, until, in a taste of what was to come in his son's career, he was overthrown a few months later by a coalition of rivals from different sides of the political spectrum. But his fortunes changed when Maximilian, House of Hapsburg, came to Mexico in 1864 to preside over a conservative government under French military protection. After a personal interview with Maximilian, the elder López Portillo went on to occupy a variety of high-level functions between May 1864 and July 1867. At the same time, the future novelist's mother was one of the ladies-in-waiting for Maximilian's Belgian wife, Carlota, sister of King Leopold, the man who so cruelly exploited the African Congo for his own enrichment. Like many collaborators, the elder López Portillo fell from grace when national resistance leader Benito Juárez returned to power in 1867. The patrician was neither exiled nor executed but instead placed under house arrest in Guadalajara. His son and future author José would have been seventeen years old at the time of his father's fall and hence internalized an awareness of the dangers of political life . . . or at least should have.[8]

"*Para todo mal, mezcal, para todo bien, también.*" So runs the refrain: "Mezcal for the bad times, but also for the good ones."[9] As the preceding thumbnail account of his forebears' lives suggests, the young José López Portillo grew up in times so tempestuous that he would need more than a shot of tequila to make his way through them. He received basic education at the local seminary and while stories of him editing the school newspaper at age twelve are almost certainly false, he did demonstrate an early aptitude for letters. National-minded liberals may have won the war decisively, but tempers still ran high in the late 1860s. Retribution killings, kangaroo courts, agrarian insurgencies, and plain old banditry all abounded; under the circumstances it was best to get the boy out of the country. José López Portillo was thus trundled off to a series of travels in the United States, Great Britain, France, Italy, and the Middle East. Such experiences removed him even further from the role of man of the people, but they did provide him with a perspective far broader than what was available to his father's generation.[10] On these travels he would have beheld great cities with astonishing displays of railroads, telegraphs, gaslights, museums, parks, department stores, voluminous print culture, and multistory constructions that seemed to touch the sky—all gifts of the industrial revolutions that at long last had made western society a serious competitor to the storied wealth of East Asia. Small wonder that a young man of those times might return to Mexico with dreams of a better way to live.

The Lure of Politics

A changing Mexico welcomed back young José López Portillo y Rojas in the early 1870s. Triumphant liberals vied with one another for leadership between 1867 and 1876, but eventually a Oaxacan general named Porfirio Díaz Mory (1835–1915) came out on top and would dominate Mexican society until 1911. Díaz liked peace and progress but strongly disapproved of political parties, as did most Mexican elites; after all, parties smacked of the rancor that had nearly torn the country apart. During the so-called Porfiriato of 1876–1911, the country thus developed a series of unwritten rules of conduct. First, no one could challenge Díaz. He occupied the role of democratic king, a man with liberal bona fides but still the final authority on anything that really mattered. Second, elections did indeed take place but with the winning candidate chosen safely in advance. Third, those expressing dissent or rival interests hived off into informal alliances centered around some charismatic if secondary figure, perhaps a powerful minister or a state governor, but never challenging the dictator himself. Stability was the Porfirian watchword, and to jeopardize that stability was akin to threatening a hive of bees.[11]

López Portillo y Rojas found his footing in this world. Like most Porfirian letrados, he studied law, but he also began writing immediately, starting with an 1874 memoir of his travels. His reputation continued to grow in spite of the occasional contretemps, and the bulk of his output, including the selections found here, emerged over the next quarter century. In 1898 López Portillo published his main and previously mentioned literary work, a sprawling, more than five-hundred-page novel entitled *La parcela.* It recounts the struggles to control a piece of land in rural Jalisco, and, while opinions differ regarding the accuracy of its portrait of country life (not exactly the author's natural habitat), it was good enough to get him elected to the Mexican Academy of Languages eight years later. His association with that body would endure for the next two decades.[12]

Having built his credentials on law and literature, he next proceeded to involve himself in politics. Like the Tabascan letrado Manuel Sánchez Mármol, López Portillo took an active role in the construction of the post-1867 order. He served several terms as *diputado federal* (the equivalent of a House of Representatives member, right down to the two-year term) and in national affairs sided with Díaz's 1876 rival Sebastián Lerdo de Tejada, a hard-core liberal but a man of law and letters, much like López Portillo himself. When Díaz triumphed, the Guadalajaran had to resign and return to his home city, but within four years all was forgiven; he reentered federal politics and even made it to the Senate. Díaz found López Portillo effective enough to be a potential challenger, so he kept the Guadalajaran close as a way of controlling his influence and ambitions.

As the regime matured, two different *camarillas*, or political factions, emerged. On one side there were old-guard Díaz men who had risen with their Oaxacan caudillo in the Reform War; they enjoyed popular, often military roots, and they found their leader in Monterrey-based strongman, Bernardo Reyes (1850–1913). The so-called *científicos*, or men of science, meanwhile, were a new breed; their claim to authority rested on technical knowledge, and they found their voice in Yucatecan man of letters and education minister Justo Sierra Méndez (1848–1912) and finance minister José Ives Limantour (1854–1935), the latter born in Mexico to a family of French land speculators. At first glance López Portillo might seem to have been destined for aligning with the científicos, but his devout Catholicism limited his embrace of positivist ideals, which required humankind to pass out of the so-called religious and metaphysical phases and into the scientific age. Perhaps more importantly, he had long and close ties to Reyes, a fellow Guadalajaran born in the same year, a man whom López Portillo had known from childhood. Shared province of origin could carry almost as much weight as blood ties in Mexican politics.

Though only fifteen years younger than Díaz, Reyes saw himself as the caudillo's natural successor; he was a loyal officer, a man with solid liberal credentials, and a miracle worker who had turned Monterrey from a dusty cowtown to an industrial hub, exactly the kind of changes Porfirians loved. To contain his ambitions, the dictator brought Reyes to the capital and appointed him minister of war in 1900–2, with López

Portillo as his secretary. When Reyes returned to govern Monterrey the following year, Díaz sent the Guadalajara novelist with him, essentially to keep an eye on a possible rival. But this hardly endangered the close relationship of the two Tapatíos. When Reyes was accused of using excessive violence to put down striking workers in 1903, it was López Portillo who successfully defended him before the Mexican congress.[13] Throughout this entire time, López Portillo successfully straddled two different loyalties, remaining committed to his friend and hero in Monterrey but serving as a fawning press agent for the president himself.

Mexican politics continued, but the dictator's life and reign most decidedly could not. When an aging Díaz's grip weakened after the 1907 economic downturn and an ill-advised foreign interview a year later, López Portillo, together with Manuel Sánchez Mármol, launched a pro-Reyes campaign, going so far as to purchase the newspaper *México Nuevo* to convert into a press mouthpiece. For his pains López Portillo found himself accused (probably by científico enemies) of fraud and embezzlement. But his fortunes changed abruptly when Díaz was driven from office in May 1911. A grateful López Portillo went so far as to write a biography of the victorious revolutionary leader, Francisco I. Madero, although in fact the book is more a rearguard condemnation of Díaz than an homage to the Apostle of Democracy. During the six-month interim government that followed, López Portillo became subsecretary of Instrucción Pública y Bellas Artes, under interim president Francisco Vásquez Gómez, but when Madero finally assumed the executive office in November of that year, López Portillo chose to return to his beloved Guadalajara and try once again for the Jalisco governorship, this time under a restructured Liberal Party clustered around the candidate himself: *liberales portillistas*.[14]

In that campaign he reaped the advantage of having suffered Díaz's persecution, but what really made the difference in the 1912 elections was an alliance with a new force: the Jalisco chapter of the Partido Católico Nacional (PCN). Pope Leo XIII's 1893 *Rerum novarum* papal bull had laid the groundwork for a socially active church that would be responsive to new working-class needs while carefully sidestepping radical alternatives, such as Marxism or anarchism. The Porfirian order had grown tolerant of religion in its last two decades, and *Rerum novarum* found a ready audience in Mexico, where it spoke to an increasingly urban laity. With the fall of Díaz it became possible to found religiously based political parties, and so the PCN was born, first in Puebla, and then chapters springing up elsewhere later.

Jalisco's PCN maintained considerable autonomy from the national umbrella organization. It drew from a heterogeneous constituency, rolled off reams of publications, championed milquetoast solutions to problems of labor and land rights, disdained Madero, and inevitably worked its way into politics. López Portillo's ideological commitment to the PCN's causes is somewhat murky; after all, he identified with the victors of the mid-century wars, a prerequisite posture for all the era's statesmen, and yet he remained decidedly Catholic, the very picture of the Porfirian liberal-conservative synthesis. He ran as candidate of the more mainstream Liberal Party, and his later actions regarding the PCN suggest a tactical alliance of uncertain commitment on his part.[15] José López Portillo had at long last won the governorship; little did he realize that he was about to enter the most turbulent and physically dangerous period of his life.

It was the worst possible time for such a victory. With Díaz gone and Madero in the Palacio Nacional, Mexico found itself torn apart by irreconcilable agendas. Those who had supported Madero's revolution—groups like disenfranchised sharecroppers in Chihuahua and the impoverished Zapatistas of Morelos—sought an end to petty rural tyrannies and an immediate rollback of the last decade of land grabs on the part of *hacendados*, the owners of the great estates. Urban workers clamored for improved conditions and the right to organize. The PCN was now at the height of its power and sought nothing less than the mainstreaming of religiously based politics, something that Madero rejected. Moreover, neither Madero nor the Catholics had any interest in radicalism. Probably the best way to categorize López Portillo was as center-right: Catholic but not religiously strident, positivist but not punitive, glad to see a revolution dethroning Díaz and yet fundamentally uninterested in wrenching issues like land reform, labor rights, rent control, anti-US nationalism, and changing gender roles, and certainly not the sort of petit bourgeois anticlericalism that informed so many of the events in the southeast.

The letrado's fortunes changed dramatically in February 1913, when Gen. Victoriano Huerta usurped the presidency after betraying and then assassinating Madero. Writing twenty-five years after the event, historian Henry Bamford Parkes characterized Huerta as "a villain on an Elizabethan scale"; modern accounts do little to soften that judgment.[16] A hard-core alcoholic, Huerta presided over an itinerant urban government, moving from bar to bar to avoid being murdered. He never understood that Porfirio Díaz operated his dictatorship more by cooptation and flexibility than by an iron fist. Lacking political skills, the general turned chief executive simply executed congressmen who disagreed with him. Unsurprisingly, Huerta himself fell after a little more than a year, victim of national outrage in the form of revolutionary caudillos Pancho Villa, Emiliano Zapata, and Venustiano Carranza, and those who had served Huerta found themselves ostracized for life.

But for a moment, at least, the Huerta regime seemed to offer safe harbor for conservative Mexicans. Thinking that circumstances had turned in their favor, Jalisco PCN members adopted a tactic that would generate no end of problems for the next twenty years: a march to crown Jesus the king of Mexico. López Portillo had originally given his approval, but at the last minute he got cold feet about going through with so blatant a display of religious assertiveness; after all, the 1857 Constitution still served as the law of the land, and it prohibited religious services outside of a church. And although the march was technically not a service, it was close enough to leave him feeling exposed. Governor López Portillo recognized the danger presented by angry marches and blatant outdoor manifestations of Catholicism. He thus issued a waffly ruling: women and children could march (they being considered entities outside of real politics), but men could not. The decision satisfied no one, and at the critical moment on January 6, 1914, the archbishop himself donned his clerical garb and led the decidedly mixed company as it paraded some twenty-five city blocks of downtown Guadalajara. Unfortunately, the event proved an embarrassment for López Portillo, as it ended in an extremely public shouting match with old-school liberal antagonists.[17]

Compared with the bloody mayhem in other parts of Mexico, a few noisy Catholics striding the streets of Guadalajara should have seemed laughable. But Huerta knew that his regime, tainted as it was with usurpation and murder, lacked all legitimacy. He also understood that, even under calmer circumstances, the smallest rumpus could explode into major violence. He forcibly repressed the march and outlawed Jalisco's Catholic Party. An otherwise reliable base of support thus vanished. For good measure, Huerta called José López Portillo to Mexico City to serve as the secretary of Foreign Relations, perhaps because he somehow trusted him or perhaps because he wanted to keep a bloodshot eye on the politician-novelist. Or perhaps it was because of a coincidental occurrence a few years earlier. López Portillo had attended an ill-fated Pan-American conference in Buenos Aires in 1910, then authored an essay two years later attacking the Monroe Doctrine, the favored device of the powerful US government, which was withholding arms and recognition from the beleaguered Huerta.[18]

In his famous archaeology of the letrados, Ángel Rama damningly asserted that Latin American men of letters, fearing eclipse from power and fearing even more the wrath of the underclasses, sided with Victoriano Huerta and his ilk.[19] Rama named no names, but one must suspect that he had José López Portillo y Rojas in mind, given how perfectly the latter fit the description. Of López Portillo's motives at this point we know little. Revolutions are hell for moderates, and it is possible that the novelist turned politician hoped that Huerta's iron fist could make some of the Madero-era unrest go away. Or perhaps he simply feared the consequences of saying no. But whatever the Tapatío writer's motivations, he stood by Huerta as long as Huerta stayed in office.

It was a costly decision. As the literati-politician learned to his regret, the job had become the hottest of potatoes. US President Woodrow Wilson listened to both his schoolmaster conscience and the entreaties of US oil companies to deny recognition, a measure that all but guaranteed Huerta's fall. Not content with diplomatic blows, Wilson then launched a prearranged plan to invade and occupy the port of Veracruz to force Huerta's abdication and as a preliminary toward forcing some sort of resolution to the welter of competing armies and caudillos. It was the first time since 1867 that Mexico had faced a serious foreign military intervention.

López Portillo y Rojas conducted much of the diplomatic communication that one reads about in connection with this affair. He made a trip to Veracruz to personally negotiate with Wilson's special envoy John Lind. But it was all to no avail; in this instance, power grew out of the barrel of a gunboat, and the United States remained firmly in control of Mexico's main port. And if we are to believe the biographical information in *Cancilleres de México*, it fell to poor López Portillo to explain to Huerta—alcoholic, desperate, and notoriously homicidal—that the game was up and that it was time for the president to step down. This Huerta did, boarding a train for Veracruz to the awaiting *Iparango*, the very same steamship that had taken Porfirio Diaz into exile to France three years earlier. The now former secretary of Foreign Relations left the capital and returned to Guadalajara to await safer times.

By 1916 López Portillo had fought the good fight. He had received a fine education, traveled the world, published extensively, risen in politics to become advisor to Díaz, pivoted to the revolutionary side, won a governorship, pivoted back to the counter-revolution, survived association with one of Mexico's darkest figures, brokered between Mexico and her invader, and like Ulysses somehow returned home to tell about it. But this time he bid adieu to politics once and for all. For once the Tapatío's timing was spot-on: he left the public sphere just as the confusing struggle that involved Venustiano Carranza, Francisco Villa, and Emiliano Zapata was reaching its height. Taking advantage of an amnesty offer by General Pablo González, José López Portillo y Rojas retired to a position in the Academy of Arts and Letters in Guadalajara. He died of kidney stones seven year later, in 1923, just as a wrenching conflict between church and state was beginning to engulf Jalisco, Michoacán, and other western states.

López Portillo as Literary Stylist

López Portillo the writer, a life-long resident of Mexico's second city, inherited a significant literary tradition. Guadalajara and nearby Lagos produced several important writers in the years following independence. These included the Franciscan historian Francisco Freijes, romantic poet Fernando Calderón, journalist José Rosas Moreno, and the multifaceted author and pro-liberal militant Ireneo Paz, grandfather of Nobel prize winner Octavio Paz. La Esperanza (Hope), the state's first literary society, was formed in 1852, when José López Portillo was a mere two years old. It produced *La falange de estudios*, the region's first literary journal. La Esperanza hosted meetings that indiscriminately blended literature, scientific presentations, and loads of superheated politics, a formula that successor organizations faithfully reproduced. The year 1866 witnessed the birth of the most important *Falange* legatees, *La República Literaria*, which would define western Mexico letters for the next thirty-two years. It was in this venue that many of López Portillo's works appear, including the short stories found here.[20]

Beyond his early memoir of travel, there are no autobiographical statements about José López Portillo y Rojas, but to judge by what does survive, he focused most of his youthful attention on writing. Was he a good writer? In many ways, yes. The works contained here contain key elements of successful fiction. They evoke a time and place. They establish individual human character. They offer a rich vocabulary. They progress when they need to and step back to reflect at exactly that moment when the reader needs time to think. Moreover, and as argued at length below, López Portillo had a knack for working the grand issues of Porfirian times into his fiction, be it in the message-laden *Nieves*, or hidden in short stories seemingly crafted for entertainment value. His writings are at times social (tales of a Mexico going through unprecedented changes) and at other moments personal (engaging with issues rooted deep in the author's personal experience). Although he was certainly a learned man, a fact evidenced in all four selections, López Portillo was also something of a prose purist. He avoided authorial intrusions in the form of footnotes; indeed, all notes found in this collection are my own, with only two exceptions, both indicated as [López Portillo's note:].

Appropriateness of content has been an issue. In an often-cited study, Roland Grass (1970) criticizes the incorporation of certain descriptive passages in the novella *Nieves*, arguing that they fail to advance the plot or bring intellectual depth to the story. Grass deserves much credit for almost single-handedly bringing critical attention to López Portillo, but that fact necessarily involved writing in a complete vacuum, and subsequent critics have questioned several of his conclusions. The digression issue, I think, is one place where Grass stumbles. His complaint about the three passages in question—descent through the canyon, the rural Jalisco rodeo, and the tequila industry—might not advance the story directly, but each has an important symbolic brief.

As for the first passage, we must recall that literary departures from the city (civilization, if one prefers) often do denote passage to a different moral world. Unclothed violence and savagery have long adorned "territorial" narratives, be they of the United States's Wild West (*The Man Who Shot Liberty Valence* [film, 1962, based on a story of the same name published in 1953]), the Amazonian interior (*La vorágine* [1924], *Doña Barbara* [1929]), the Argentine pampas (*Facundo* [1845]), and in what may be the most memorable colonial critique of all, featuring sub-Saharan Africa (*Heart of Darkness* [1899]). The list is long. Indeed, the vision of territories as places of moral atavism runs so deep that Rudyard Kipling spoke for many colonials when, in his poem "Mandalay," he described Burma as a place "where there aren't no Ten Commandments."

In the case of *Nieves*, however, the change is salutary, even refreshing. If Don Santos's more accessibly located hacienda of La Florida represents a corrupt, fallen world, the descent to the hacienda of El Potrero and its edenic fruit orchard is clearly a return to the some purer, more pristine Mexico, a place in which virtue prevails and poverty is no barrier to connubial bliss. The descent speaks of how much one could hope to reclaim by leaving the city. If urban Porfirians saw their world as a time of progress and enlightenment, then the return to the more citified Tequila reminds us that most of the aforementioned qualities were mere façade.

The second descriptive passage involves López Portillo's account of the bullfight and rodeo, and that account is so detailed that at times it reads like an anthropologist's field notes. It is unlikely to win new fans for this now-controversial form of entertainment. A clear majority of the Mexican public now opposes bullfights, even the nonlethal variety presented here. *Corridas de toros* are currently banned in the states of Coahuila, Guerrero, Quintana Roo, Sinoloa, and Sonora. They probably would have ended long ago, had it not been for the need to make concessions to the rural sector and to the many people who earn a living off corrida-related sales and activities. But spin-off merchandise is not the point. In the narrator's world, rather, prowess in dealing with bulls and horses qualified the competitor as a real man, and winning recognition as the vaquero of vaqueros meant that the victor really did deserve the woman as his prize. It required the machinations of a malevolently narcissistic landowner to violate this accepted social order and claim that prize for himself. As Don Santos discovers, nature imposes a justice of her own. Beyond laying down the more essential symbolic turf, the passage offers some of the novella's most interesting parts, insofar as they ground the work among real people in a real place, as opposed to leaving it as nothing more than a story of average people in Anyplace, Mexico. We can probably thank López Portillo, then, for not being too conscious of word count.

López Portillo once again reads like an anthropologist transcribing his field notes when he explains in a third passage how tequila is made. This section walks readers through the origins of the liquor, its distillation in the times of his grandfather, and the innovations of the present day. The section too has a function. It pauses what by this point has become a tense, highly wrought narrative; as Charles Dickens said, "Make 'em laugh, make 'em cry, make 'em wait." It also does something essential for the novella, which is to situate once again it among real people, real places, and real-life activities. But symbolism is afoot as well. It is no accident that the anonymous narrator encounters the distraught Nieves here; recently escaped from a near-rape at the hands of Don Santos, she returns to the place that epitomizes an older, more moral world, in which the physiocrat landowner not only fostered economic development but also extended paternal protection to his employees and servants.

Even if López Portillo goes on a bit in these descriptive passages, we must grant the writer points in other areas. The dialogue is crisp and fast-paced. Action narrative passages come off as clear, even intense. López Portillo also takes on sensitive topics, such as the interplay of sex, money, and power, a point explored below. Moreover, there is something familiar in *Nieves*. A native Tapatío returning to his home property; a land haunted by memories; sexual depredation as daily pastime; a cruel hacendado who lords over his fellow *jaliscienses:* Juan Rulfo could hardly have been ignorant of *Nieves* when he wrote his

1955 bombshell *Pedro Páramo.* In sum, then, López Portillo knew his way around the written page, and if readers are willing to invest a brief amount of time in understanding the world of late nineteenth-century Mexico, they will find that the novellas like *Nieves*, together with short stories like "The Mirror," "The Lottery Ticket," and "The Bracelet," still walk that narrow path between entertainment and meaning.

López Portillo's writings are solid enough that in Mexico, at least, they have gained a place in regional memory. In 1995 the famous Artes de México series published a tequila volume, with reprints in 1999 and 2008, and quotes and citations from *Nieves* recur throughout the text.[21] More recently (2022), Guadalajara's Taller de Gráfica Comala published *El antiguo método de elaboración del vino mexcal de Tequila descrito en la novela Nieves del siglo XIX por José López Portillo y Rojas*, an annotated illustration of the novella's tequila-making process, complete with impressive woodcuts by Ignacio Gómez Arriola.[22] However, and particularly among English-language readers, López Portillo has failed to garner the widespread reputation of authors such as Ignacio Altamirano, José Joaquín Fernández de Lizardi, and Manuel Payno. It is an unfortunate reality that this anthology hopes to help redress.

Anatomy of a Rebellion

López Portillo wrote on a wide variety of themes, and like many of his contemporaries he occasionally wandered into the long ago and far away. But not here: the four works chosen for this collection have Mexico as a setting. They include a large city (Mexico City? Guadalajara?) for "The Mirror" and "The Lottery Ticket," Veracruz for "The Bracelet," and a cartographically accurate depiction of rural Jalisco for *Nieves.* They were scenes that the author knew well, and he quite ably brings them to life.

The logical place for interpretation to begin is with the largest question: what was the overall theme or issue that informed his prose? Does his corpus contain some overriding quest or question, perhaps in the way that Boom literature sought to blend the search for Latin American identity with narrative fragmentation, à la Joyce and Faulkner, sautèed with a generous helping of Kafkan surrealism?

In this collection the logical place to find an answer is with the best-known and most fully developed entry. *Nieves* (together with the far longer and more fully developed *La parcela*) have drawn more critical attention than any other work by López Portillo. In her provocative *Foundational Fictions* (1992), Doris Sommer argues that as part of their project of using fictional narrative to foster national identity, Latin America's nineteenth-century authors had to find ways to bridge class and ethnicity, the great canyons that cleaved so much of their region and that threatened to render unity impossible. Their solution, Sommer posits, often came in the form of cross-ethnic matrimony, the legal and physical bonding that spans the great gap. Wedding vows, the idea ran, might overcome the differences that constitutions could not. For example, in Ignacio Altamirano's *El Zarco* the noble and trustworthy indigenous blacksmith Nicolás eventually weds Pilar, a mestiza with dusky skin and a heart of gold. Their matrimony, it seems, serves up a metaphor for how sincere people can join together in the new liberal-operated world of Mexican nationalism.[23]

Oddly, no such message features in *Nieves*. The novella is about white people, however raggedy, marrying other white people. Nothing is bridged, and the grand canyons of class and ethnicity gape as widely as ever. The explanation, I think, turns us to authorial intention: like the famous Oscar Lewis, who compiled endless reams of data on the lives of unhappy people, always chasing a phantom that he called "the culture of poverty," López Portillo was fundamentally interested in why things went wrong, not in prescribing how to put them right again.[24] The scant existing commentary on *Nieves* focuses on whether the author was or was not a real reformer (whatever that term might entail), a question that misses the mark. As Mario Martín-Flores rightly observes when critiquing Roland Grass, there is no real reform highlighted in yellow, no proposal beyond urging people to behave themselves . . . which is no real proposal at all. But if that is true, what experience lies behind López Portillo's questioning? What was the situation that had gone so terribly awry? What exactly led the city-slicker novelist and diputado to rake up country dirt?

López Portillo plants his driving concern in the opening paragraph, right under our noses, but for some reason we have declined to pay attention. Literature often draws from the events of a real past, and in the case of *Nieves* much of the novella's historical inspiration lies in the stories and legends surrounding Jalisco's most famous rebel, Manuel Lozada. References to this inveterate rebel appear throughout the text. I suggest that just as the novel *Ánton Pérez* (1913) was author Manuel Sánchez Mármol's attempt to understand how catastrophically off-course his own life might have gone had he not been born into creole privilege, *Nieves* explores just what it was about the world of rural Jalisco that might goad a man into a life of rebellion.

It will come as no surprise to learn that the real Lozada differed considerably from López Portillo's fictional Juan, the barefoot gardener and expert bull rider.[25] Born Elpidio García González on September 22, 1828, in the town of San Luis (now part of the state of Nayarit), he was raised by an uncle, whose surname he eventually adopted. Little is known of Lozada's childhood. Of Cora Indian ancestry, Lozada grew up a servant on a hacienda, where at least in some versions he ran off with the proprietor's daughter, thus making him a marked man. In other accounts he was publicly whipped by a soldier but organized a band of followers, returned to kill his tormentor, then eloped with the daughter. Variations of this story are common enough to qualify it as a leitmotif of Mexican folklore (similar unsubstantiated accounts attached themselves to Pancho Villa and persist to the present). We have the boy of plebeian ancestry, the socially prohibited love, the public outrage, the just if brutal revenge, followed by flight to the mountains and the life of a courageous outlaw.

Less apocryphal is Lozada's later career as regional power broker. In a twist reminiscent of Billy the Kid's saga, the young Lozada was also hired as a gunman by western Jalisco's foremost mercantile concern, the formidable Barrón and Forbes Company. The relationship apparently inspired no love for either hacendados or financiers, and on September 22, 1857, Lozada's fifteen-year career as rebel began with a bloody raid on the Hacienda de Puga. Lozada now became El Tigre de Álica, a reference to the mountain redoubt in which he and his men took refuge.[26]

Patrician historians condemned Lozada as the leader of "semi-barbaric Indians known for their ferocious deeds."[27] While such deeds did take place, they came not as simple bloodlust but rather in defense of what Zachary Brittsan has called "popular conservatism," an ideological holdover from colonial days, one that blended religion, communal land rights, and local autonomy.[28] Similarly, Michele McArdle Stephens documents that the indigenous Wixacari (Huichol) and Coras found the expulsion of the Franciscans, their long-time protectors, particularly outrageous.[29] In sum, Lozada, part indigenous Cora himself, was a regional rather than national leader who spoke to needs and interests that liberal statesmen refused to recognize.

Lozada's career followed a series of shifting alliances. He eventually was on good terms with President Benito Juárez following the collapse of the French Intervention in 1867, but the alliance ended when Juárez abruptly died in 1872 and the less accommodating Sebastián Lerdo de Tejada came to power. Then, Lozada took up arms against the federal government yet again. The climax of this final campaign came on January 22, 1873, when Lozada occupied the town of Tequila and squeezed it for arms and supplies. Contrary to López Portillo's purported memory, Tequila residents mounted no successful resistance. Unfortunately for El Tigre de Álica, he fell to a superior army under Gen. Ramón Corona a mere six days later. After being captured, photographed, and tried before a military court, Lozada was passed before a firing squad and into legend on July 19.[30]

The shadow of Lozada thus hangs over much of the novella, and the character of Juan reads like a study in how a simple, good-hearted individual might have risen to rebel commander, situating that study in the author's own private recollections of the Mexican regional past. What clouds interpretation is the fact that López Portillo, like so many other Porfirian elites, was a thoroughgoing follower of positivism. A complete exploration of this philosophy is impossible here; suffice to say that it stressed a universal progression from the age of religion and myth to an age of metaphysical abstraction and finally to society's final arrival to the world of science. Only quantitative factors, such as miles of railroads or tons of silver exports, could accurately measure social advancement. Informed scientific administration had to replace politics; correlatively, positivists saw mass participation in politics as a combination of ignorance, ambition, and ill-intentioned grousing and assumed that it needed to be ignored or else forcibly suppressed. In this conservative and elitist way of thought, the poor were to blame for their poverty; perhaps it was illiteracy, perhaps malnutrition, perhaps indigenous blood, perhaps shaky hygiene. The mere idea of a Cora Indian as regional power broker understandably offended urban letrados. For all his insightful forays into Mexican society, then, López Portillo often slips back into positivist and unabashedly Europhile perspectives, thus complicating and in some cases defeating his own quest to understand why things go wrong.

Positivist distortions are evident above all in matters of ethnicity. Pigmentocracy reigns here. Latin America's seemingly endless fixation on blond, blue-eyed people is on full display. In the same way that modernist master poet Rubén Darío could remark in a short story that his cousin was "blond, and therefore sweet-tempered," the heroine-victim Nieves has to be golden-haired and blue-eyed to qualify as the sweetheart of the rodeo. The mere presence of this curiously Nordic beauty on a hardscrabble western hacienda is something the novella never bothers to explain. Pigmentocracy's grip was particularly unpardoning when it came to indigenous matters. López Portillo confines himself to a mestizo world, the only world he really understood. All biographical and textual evidence suggests that he knew next to nothing about the indigenous peoples who followed Lozada. Four major ethnic groups—Nayaarite, Wixacari (Huichol), O'dam, and Mexicanos—inhabited the region of the Grand Nayar, that sprawling obstacle course of a land that covered five western states, including much of the author's beloved Jalisco. Like the human wave that followed Miguel Hidalgo, they drew little distinction between Spaniards and creoles, resented mestizos of any sort, and did not particularly care whether hacendados behaved themselves with female servants. Lozado may have perished, but the indigenous lieutenants who served him survived, and their influence in the region lasted well into Porfirian times. None of this is evident in *Nieves*, in which the sole visibly indigenous person is a buffoonish manservant who only shows up long enough to cower before the manly, pistol-toting mestizo hero.

Nowhere does the conflict between positivism and hard-nosed investigative experience emerge more clearly than in the novella's question of banditry and revolt, two phenomena that López Portillo saw as one. His interest in the matter was hardly incidental. "*L'homme armé doibt on doubter*," ran the fifteenth-century French lyric: "Beware the armed man." Newly independent Latin Americans quickly discovered the problem amounted to more than just a troubadour's trope. Indeed, the problem of armed men (with or without social conscience) recurred regularly in early national Latin America and its literature. It fed on situations where the state and its institutions were weak, where gross inequalities prevailed, where endemic warfare whipsawed the land, and where power gravitated into the hands of strongmen. The so-called caudillo, often himself a landowner, used his wealth and social influence to raise and equip a private army for such causes as provincial autonomy and its evil twin, separatism; the righting of injustices; or simple self-enrichment. The informal nature of caudillo bands naturally tempted them to live off the people, and armed followers were known to continue their bandit ways long after the original political motivation had faded. Beware indeed the armed man. The bandit curse only subsided as financially solvent agromineral export states rose in the last third of the nineteenth century, but the writers of that same period often looked back to Latin America's time of troubles as grist for exciting fictional narratives.[31]

Tracking *l'homme armé* to his criminal lair meant full understanding of the world around him. Positivist authors have a hard-earned reputation for classist insensitivity, but López Portillo has a discerning eye for local power—absent when needed, copious when not—and his richly marbled accounts still retain their sharp focus. For starters, the author makes clear that the church is no longer the all-present stabilizing institution of colonial days; rather, it appears as a diminished force by the late 1880s, now reduced in comparison to the new gods of technology, foreign capital, and European high culture. Porfirian liberals liked their priests to be well intentioned but weak; of the people and yet overweight; fumbling, and strictly a sidebar to the real action. So it is here. Ever a man in the middle, López Portillo makes it clear that he is a positivist but not a priest hater, an intellectual but not an iconoclast.

The position of that rising star of rural governance, the *jefe político*, requires some explanation. A holdover from late colonial times, the *jefatura* was a governor-appointed position with the omnibus brief of making certain that the rural world remained peaceful and law abiding, and that the governor and president stayed informed. There is no counterpart to this office in, say, the US political system, and it grew out of the dynamics and expectations of colonial authoritarianism. Twentieth-century revolutionaries declared the jefes to be villains, despite the fact that the latter's real nature and attitudes were more complicated.[32] But there can be little doubt that jefes had to take seriously the concerns of rural proprietors. Like so much of Porfirian Mexico, these "eyes of the czar" depended on the projected image of power, and not on their real power, to keep the peace. How limited that power was becomes clear in a tight spot. Tequila's jefe politico is too close to men of property and ultimately fails in his duty to administer impartial justice. At least some of the local gentry see the jefe as an overpaid liability and are reluctant to help him defend the town against marauders, especially when it means risking their own necks.

All of which brings us back to the problem of the Porfirian hacendado. There are fewer figures of greater controversy in Latin American history, and *Nieves* gives us some idea of why. In the lost halcyon days of the seventeenth century, hacendados and their peons had to observe certain rules of behavior; after all, markets were sluggish, the hacienda was out there on its own, and people had to get along. But once the railroads came through, access to the riches of foreign markets freed hacendados from interdependence on local workers and clients. The old give-and-take gave out, and, for the first time in Mexican history, hacendados were free to treat their servants with utter disregard for any rights, traditions, or community welfare. As Friedrich Katz memorably concluded in his landmark biography of Pancho Villa, "If ever there was a system that forced men who might have had no criminal intent to become outlaws, it was the political and social structures of Porfirian Durango. Any peon who incurred the dislike of a hacendado could be sent away into the army without a hearing, a fate that in many respects was akin to slavery. Unless exceptional circumstances obtained, he had no possibility of appeal. Faced with that choice, it is not surprising that many men, especially if they were strong-willed and courageous, chose the alternative of becoming outlaws."[33]

Rural Jalisco was apparently close behind. The servants see Don Santos as a law in and of himself: the landowner, the *jefe*, the *amo*, the *patrón*, the *hacendado*, the man in the big house, or whatever one chose to call him. If Don Santos said that Juan tried to kill him and needed to be punished, the matter was settled. Porfirio Díaz countenanced such abuses, for he needed the revenues and the support, and in all likelihood because he believed there was no other way.

The author himself evinces pure contempt for Mexico's rebels. He obviously has a low opinion of armed uprisings, albeit granting some allowances for the by-then enshrined memory of Miguel Hidalgo and his revolt against Spanish rule. (Here as elsewhere, the best rebels are both virtuous and dead.) Perhaps the best way to state the matter is that the anonymous narrator sees Tequila's uprising as tragic, its leaders cynical and self serving, and its followers probably doomed to failure. He also recognizes that this is the only way that people like Juan and Nieves can obtain a modicum of justice, and the only way that malefactors like Don Santos ever get what is coming to them. By the end of the novella, then, the shoeless and un-surnamed Juan has *become* Lozada.

In sum, *Nieves* offers a complicated analysis of why things go wrong and how rebels are born. If López Portillo disdained public violence—and the only people who do not are those who have never experienced it—he also had a discerning eye for the way such violence could play out. One of the novella's other contributions in this regard is its depiction of what happened when a rebellion took place. We may question whether his account is a bit too benign. But the tension was real enough, the articulation of political platform rather vague, the opening of jails in all probability a reality, and the utter cynicism of at least some leaders a reasonably safe bet.

Poverty amid Progress

The natural concomitant to a land of broken institutions and shoddy morals was poverty, both as their cause and their effect. We have already seen how rural disparities of resources afflict the world of *Nieves*. Elsewhere in this volume, the short story "The Lottery Ticket" approaches the matter from a slightly different angle. It too catches López Portillo in the crossfire of his own mixed emotions. On one hand this story of a luckless couple robbed of their only hope reveals deeply positivist tendencies: poverty exists because some people are simply not up to the competition for survival. On the other hand, there is a caustic awareness of the way that affluent and overbearing Porfirians could throw their weight around, rising as a clear result of others' misfortunes and then attributing it all to their own virtue and industry.

The institution on which "The Lottery Ticket" is based has a long vintage in Latin America, where it still occupies a central role in matters of both public finances and popular consciousness. In fact, Spanish Bourbon reformers introduced national lottery drawings in Mexico in 1771 as a way of addressing two different concerns. Their first motive derived from the Enlightenment state's campaign to replace popular games of chance with something more stable and controlled; the second was that the Spanish empire's notorious and perennial cash shortage loomed in the background. Tickets were originally costly, the playthings of gentlemen, but experimentation quickly showed that cheaper tickets meant more purchasers and consequently greater revenues for projects of benevolence, education, and defense. This realization in turn brought the lottery down to the level of common citizens. Despite political instability, recurring competition from private raffles, and an extended period of administration by the San Carlos art academy, the practice endured into the national period, achieving an apotheosis of sorts in 1861, when President Benito Juárez renationalized control. Pre-Porfirian governments tried using lottery revenues to construct a national railroad network, at least until those revenues proved hopelessly unequal to the task. Don Porfirio eventually fell, a national revolution raged, and Mexicans spent upward of twenty years searching for a new order, but all along the way the people's willingness to bet a few pesos on a brighter future stayed strong. Lotto fever was here to stay.[34]

Then as now, selling tickets of hope provided a means for financing various aspects of government in a society in which the rich paid few taxes and the poor lacked any means to do so. Even today, Mexico is a low-tax society compared with the United States. Special fees substitute, but for those special projects, such as education, hospitals, and charities, Latin America has often relied on lottery tickets. Administrators can defend the approach for its effectiveness: people will happily part with their money for some things, not for others. Many years ago anthropologist George Foster attributed this fact to what he called the peasant concept of "the limited good," wherein the good things of the earth were all taken and that for anyone to get ahead, luck and opportunity had to come from circumstances outside of one's own profession and family . . . like winning Powerball, for example.[35] Foster was thinking of peasant societies, but his ideas have just as much relevance for the huddled urban masses of "The Lottery Ticket."

Beyond meditating over the dynamics of poverty and success, "The Lottery Ticket" throws out tidbits that link it to turn-of-the-century Mexico. Significantly, a Spaniard and not a Mexican operates the local pawnshop, a reminder that colonial roles tended to outlive the empire's fall. In the person of Blas, a hopelessly ineffective dreamer lost in horticultural experiments, López Portillo might well be taking a swipe at would-be agrarian reformers, a group with whom he manifested little sympathy in his own life and political career. To be fair, throughout the story he does reveal an awareness of the plight of Mexico's urban poor, one of the fastest-growing classes in all the Porfiriato, a time when increasing land values and legal manipulations allowed commercial investors to gobble up vast amounts of acreage. Many of the dispossessed fled to the larger cities, where the nascent industrial and service sectors were still incapable of absorbing them. They congregated in tenements carved out of old colonial houses, places where everyone knew everyone else's business, where goats and chickens gamboled on the patio, and where the women always had laundry hanging out to dry. Here an odd job was often the only job. Urban down-and-outers have remained a standard fixture ever after; they inhabit not only reality itself but in fact constitute their own separate genre within Mexican literature. Narratives of city poverty begin with Joaquín de Fernández Lizardi's *El periquillo sarniento* (1816), and while Manuel Payno's *Los bandidos de Río Frío* (1891) is commonly regarded as a tale of the countryside, an appreciable part of its sprawling story takes place in Mexico City. The tradition acquired strength with the huge post-1950 exodus to the cities and includes modern novels such as Armando Ramírez's gritty *Chin Chin el Teporocho* (1971). Urban down-and-outers also form the basis of (again) Oscar Lewis's memorable and genre-defying *The Children of Sánchez* (1961), in which the sons and daughters of a hard-working campesino turned janitor continually find new ways to defeat themselves. Finally, the genre adapted quite naturally to the big screen. We find it in the golden age of Mexican cinema, with such much-loved films as the Cantinflas breakout *Allí está el detalle* (1940) and the Pedro Infante vehicle *Nosotros los pobres* (1948), and the theme stretches into the twenty-first century in the hard-hitting *Amores Perros* (2000) and comedies like *Nosotros los Nobles* (2013).

A careful reading of "The Lottery Ticket" suggests that López Portillo struggled to find a balance between message and plot line. Indeed, the story's overall effectiveness depends on a single and not entirely clear detail: at what moment did snooty sister Damiana become aware of the winning lottery number? If, as a tightly literal reading might suggest, she only learned of it after her confrontation with sister Genoveva, then the whole story becomes a tale of frustrating coincidence, deepened only by the pathos López Portillo endows to Genoveva: the pusillanimous poor versus the rapacious if fundamentally lucky rich. If, however, Damiana already knew that Blas and Genoveva held the winning ticket, then the story becomes a much harsher condemnation of the Porfiran upper class. Arguing in favor of this second reading are the story's chronology and the utterly flimsy excuse Damiana plies to get Blas to exchange tickets. Then who is to blame? Perhaps the ambiguities of plot construction reflected the author's own deeply ambivalent attitudes toward his world. These attitudes suggest an awareness of the injustices of society, but a reluctance to a full-on condemnation of the privileged classes to which he himself belonged. Was it all, as historian Juan José Reyes put it, "*una cuestión de suerte*" (a question of luck)? Or is something deeper afoot? López Portillo advances no solution as Blas Carranza and his wife lose big and wander into obscurity. The story's more redeeming features consist in its capture of social dynamics and in the tragic impotence of those who lost out in the great Porfirian struggle for mobility.

Holding on to Yesterday

To compartmentalize López Portillo as a writer of sentimental literature is true in some ways, false in others. Upon reading the opening paragraphs of "The Mirror," readers are apt to think that they have stepped deep into the nineteenth-century's mud puddle of overblown emotion, a world of histrionic personalities where everyone spends their lives alternately rejoicing and gnashing their teeth. But it is more complicated than that. The conditions of López Portillo's long life were often so challenging that one wonders how to reconcile them with the conventions of sentimentality so common in poems and stories of the time. Indeed, perhaps he and other literary artists found in literary mannerism a pomade for the abrasions of real life. Social conflicts and psychological torments are never far from the surface in nearly all his works and often become focal points. Such is the case here.

Nostalgia features prominently in this collection. Indeed, its narratives convey a strong sense that rural Jalisco's better days are now behind it. In *Nieves*, the initial recollections of the narrator's grandfather—rich, hard-working, and benevolent as old Saint Nick—underscore the fact that we are now dealing with a collection of predators and opportunists. The law is a dead ancestor, revered in word and ceremony but ignored in actual practice. The narrator, presumably reflecting the view of López Portillo himself, expressly blames Mexico's mid-century wars for destroying his grandfather's lucrative tequila industry. That perception of the Jalisco economy was accurate, at least heading out of the 1870s.[36]

But the perception that things were better in the old days, that air of fallenness that lingers throughout *Nieves*, begs clarification. The perceptions that inform the novella catch Jalisco society in the doldrums left over from the Reform Wars and just before the economic revitalization that took place under Díaz. Regarding La Rojeña, the hacienda portrayed in *Nieves*, López Portillo takes inspiration from the twenty years between the death of Don Vicente (1868) and the beginning of economic revitalization under his nephew Jesús Flores (1888). *Nieves* in fact gives us some idea of how the family business struggled in those years and why his mother and aunt were willing to cede their estate to their cousin, who had already become a successful manager of tequila concerns. Indeed, better days were on the way even as the author set pen to paper. The region was about to experience impressive growth in its role as one of Mexico's basic grain baskets and cattle centers. Mining would prosper as well, fueled here as elsewhere by foreign investment. It is true that Jalisco, together with several other surrounding western states, never became a motor of the economy; rather, it suffered in the shade of mining regions, like Chihuahua and Sonora or the Veracruz petroleum fields, and of key agroexports, like Chiapan coffee, Coahuila's cotton and guayule, and Yucatán's henequen. But Jalisco did play a major hand in feeding the rest of Mexico, and in 1883 it was far too early to catch some whiff of gangrene in the Porfirian system. Indeed, two decades would have to pass before prerevolutionary malaise troubled the economy.[37]

The tequila business was booming at this time. In the second half of the century, tequila distillers launched massively successful export campaigns to the lucrative United States market, stoked in particular by the growth of California. Barrels rolled out and money rolled in, and when it became clear that a more accessible approach was needed, companies like José Cuervo and rival Suaza began to ship out tequila in specially blown glass bottles ideal for individual tippling. More importantly, post-1850 planters systematically removed diverse heirloom varieties in favor of blue agave (believed to have been first encountered growing in the very canyon that the author so lovingly describes). By the mid-1900s the famous blue agave accounted for over 90 percent of all production. This relentlessly unvaried monoculture carried the usual blowback, and by the 1980s mass vulnerability to parasites and viruses had begun to take its toll. Most "100 percent blue agave" tequila consumed today is 51 percent or slightly higher, and the future of the industry as we know it may well depend on genetically modified species, combined with some form of return to biodiversity.[38]

Of course, a thirty-three-year-old López Portillo could not have foreseen these twists and complications. His sense of angst probably derived less from the loss of family fortunes, but rather from the wistfulness that usually accompanies restructuring. Neither López Portillo nor his father made a living in the field; rather, they worked the urban sphere, dealing in politics, literature, and legal and civil service, and if the López Portillo saw haciendas like El Rojeño at all, he did so during vacation getaways like the one described in *Nieves*. Life was now easier, cleaner, more cosmopolitan, and perhaps even happier, but still something had been lost. The days of venerable old Don Vicente had gone forever, and with them the life of the nobleman landowner. Only depraved mutations like Don Santos survived, creeping about fields and huts like some half-human predators.

López Portillo holds on to these ghosts of yesteryear. He is often described as a realist author (realism perhaps best conceived as sentimentality's dark twin), but if works like "The Mirror" ("El espejo") are considered, it may not be a reality any of us care to inhabit. "The Mirror" suggests an interesting combination of influences. Initially the reader gets a taste of that ripe emotion that reached its pinnacle in turn-of-the-century Latin America's best-selling novel, *María*. López Portillo hits the sentimental high notes. Present too is the death cult in which fair-haired maidens fade away from some undiagnosable wasting disease, taking their time so as to make everyone as sad and distraught as possible. (Recall that in Bram Stoker's *Dracula*, published in 1897, a mere ten years after *Nieves*, the supernaturally afflicted Lucy takes dozens of pages to finally die and become a vampire.)

However, it is Edgar Allen Poe's fingerprints that we find everywhere in this story: a drafty old house, a young man of morbid hypersensitivity, strange sights and sounds late at night, and a dying wife who manifests a bit too much interest in what her husband will do after she passes to the other side. Indeed, if *Nieves* and "The Bracelet" explore lives haunted by memories, then "The Mirror" lays out a tale that would have satisfied that high priest of Latin American Poe-ism, Horacio Quiroga.

To what degree did classic horror stories come from the author's own inner demons? And was "The Mirror" somehow autobiographical? Most evidence suggests that Edgar Allen Poe took a rather workmanlike approach to his craft. If Quiroga was haunted by his family's extensive history of suicides and by the impenetrable Amazonian rainforest; and if E. T. A. Hoffmann struggled with poverty, alcoholism, syphilis, and Napoleonic invasions; and if one at times wonders about the sanity of horror-master H. P. Lovecraft, then Poe himself dispels those notions in his self-mocking "How to Write a Blackwood Article." Learn the formula and churn 'em out, he advises an aspiring young author.[39] In fact, much of the "spooky" image of Poe derives from his prose, from his somber photos, and from his mysterious death in 1849.

But in López Portillo's case, the story of the dying young wife and her complicated legacy to the survivors may have come from somewhere closer to the heart. José López Portillo's first wife, María de

Jesús Gómez y Luna, died in 1878, after only a few years of marriage, at the tender age of twenty-four, while their child, a baby boy, died in infancy. (Interestingly enough, the word *luna,* his late wife's second patronymic, recurs throughout the story, and with multiple meanings.) Like the anonymous narrator of "The Mirror," the now-widowed López Portillo doubtless struggled with emotions of loss and a sense of betrayal, issues that he appeared to overcome six years later with his second marriage, this time to Tepic-born Margarita Weber Narváez, the woman who would bear their children and avoided an early demise: she lived on to become the venerated family matriarch, dying in 1960 at the age of one hundred.

Dramas of the Heart

Finally, and perhaps most importantly, López Portillo works the theme of love, not exclusively as the sugar coating of romance novels, but also a grittier love, one that entails pregnancies, burdensome children, predatory patrons, and destructive obsessions, among other problems. Love is a blessing, a curse, and a crucifixion, a gift to be treasured but also a commodity to be traded, like money and influence.

Nowhere are the many variations of sex, love, and power more evident here than in *Nieves,* where they constitute a key narrative motor. Indeed, even jaded twenty-first century readers are apt to be shocked by the novella's exploration of this rural world's blatant sexism and horrendous rape culture. *Nieves* begins as a nostalgic memoir, but shortly into the second section events take an unsettling turn, when Don Santos invites the anonymous narrator to accompany him on a "skin tour" of the former's estate. At times the narrative of *Nieves* reads like pedophilia, but this was a world where rural boys married as soon as they could farm or ranch, while girls often wed as soon as they reached puberty, it being their fate in life to produce many, many children. After all, they knew that most of them might die before attaining their majority. But even in these circumstances, Don Santos's lust for poor young Nieves is clearly out of bounds, and his attempt to monopolize the young woman for himself is the motor of radicalization here. This narrative strategy can illuminate, and it can also disappoint. On one hand, López Portillo exposes a seamy side of Mexico's hacienda system, one that few other of his contemporaries took on with such candor. On the other hand, presenting sexual abuse as the motive for radicalization comes up short; the reader immediately connects with poor Nieves and her outlaw lover Juan, but advancing this abuse as the reason for enduring, large-scale insurgencies is a bit like attributing the Trojan War to Helen's abduction: clear and simple, if utterly insufficient from the historian's point of view.

In terms of love interest, perhaps the hardest character to fathom in *Nieves* is the narrator himself. Indeed, the unnamed López Portillo surrogate takes an uncomfortably long time to distance himself from the predatory pedophilia that raged on the property of Don Santos. His initial silence may indicate just how acceptable such attitudes were, at least as long as the girls in question remained eye candy and not real physical conquests. At times it appears that he too finds Nieves attractive, but this may reflect nothing more than the obvious fact that positivist gentlemen prefer blondes. At other times the narrative takes on a strangely homoerotic quality, as in the description of the bath outside the El Potrero hacienda. The narrator is neither a revolutionary nor at one with the rural world, a place that he has clearly left behind, and which for all its lush beauty and golden memories (or perhaps because of those memories) it now pains him to see.

The best reading, I think, is that he sees himself as fundamentally above this rural world, with its underdevelopment, its unpredictability, and its moral squalor, and he permits himself to take little more than an observer's role in events. His decision to extend a limited if helping hand to the young couple ultimately contributes to the couple's decision to become insurgents. Is the implication, then, that things are going to go wrong, no matter what, and that it is best not to get involved, romantically or otherwise?

It would be easy enough to label López Portillo as a caveman in terms of gender issues, but the fact is he did manage to put his finger on one important dilemma: poor women had few options, and while poor *beautiful* women may have fared a bit better, by the same token they came under pressures of their own. The link between social power and sexual abuse was real enough, and this may be the novella's greatest contribution to expanding our consciousness of the time and place.

Among the more depressing elements of the story is the way Nieves's family is willing to hand her over to Don Santos's desires as a way of improving their own position on the hacienda.

A second common feature of these works is that they deal with issues of the time, particularly the immense and often arbitrary power that the rich wielded over the poor. Even "The Bracelet," which is beyond doubt the more personal and introspective of the three short stories here, offers a nod of recognition to the constricting roles and options available for women of the time (a theme explored deeply in *Nieves,* but here raised more as background material than social issue).

Juan's idea of carrying off Nieves reflected actual practice. Known in legal circles as *rapto,* it was a way of circumventing parental opposition by presenting the angry father and mother with a fait accompli. It involved a pretense that the man had carried off the intended bride and supposedly against her will. With the woman's and her family's honor now gravely damaged, the only way to make amends was for the offending suitor to "go ahead and marry the gal."[40] This elaborate social pantomime turns up in Spanish-language literature as far back as the ground-breaking *La Celestina* of 1499.

The final selection here returns us to this most abiding of López Portillo's obsessions: love, sometimes pure and spiritual, sometimes erotic, but almost always frustrated. "The Bracelet" ("El brazalete") takes place in Veracruz, that sultry and idyllic port city that Mexico City–born Agustín Lara made his imaginary hometown, a place where the melodies of *son jarocho* forever spill into the plazas, and where a waiter with *café con leche* is always listening for that tap of the spoon on the empty glass that summons him to the table. In this case, however, the action takes place at the level of well-to-do visitors: the Guadalajara narrator (Enrique) and a young woman of Havana (Rita). Their scenes are balconies of hotels and the railed platforms of steamships. Neither of them works because neither of them needs to work; there is no poverty here.

This story brings together several of the themes explored above and also provides one of López Portillo's best-ever endings, something that I think qualifies it as the piece to close the collection. Poetic impact aside, it leaves us with a question that admits no easy answer. Who is more at fault here: a possessive young man who insists on controlling his lover's past, or the young woman who refuses to let go of that past, however painful and destructive it may be? It offers an interesting companion story to "The Mirror," only now scrubbed of any sort of paranormal overtones. López Portillo strips the narrative down to human passion at its most stubborn and self-defeating. A ghost of a different sort walks these pages. More psychological than ectoplasmic, it signals basic human inability to forget the trauma of lovers lost and times gone by.

Forgetting trauma is healthy and recommended; forgetting a major author is neither. José López Portillo y Rojas made an outstanding contribution to Mexican and Latin American letters, and for some reason we have relegated him to the high, dusty shelf of lesser writers. Perhaps it was the Revolution's cultural battle cry of "out with the old." Perhaps it was discomfort with the frequently awful nineteenth century. Perhaps, as Doris Sommer put it, we fell for the Boom writers' tendentious claim that nothing printed before them was really worth reading.[41] An older generation of English-language scholars, enamored by what historian Helen Delpar called the Revolution-inspired "enormous vogue of things Mexican," certainly bought that line, and if they accorded any critical space at all to López Portillo and his contemporaries, they did so as part of a brief introductory chapter that saw anything before writers B. Traven, Mariano Azuela, Juan Rulfo, and Carlos Fuentes as mere warm-up.[42] This collection offers a small sample of the Tapatío's sprawling corpus of novels, novellas, short stories, travel memoirs, and poetry. But in so doing it leaves us, I hope, with a message: Porfirians saw José López Portillo y Rojas as standing in the forefront of their national literature for good reasons. His creative legacy lives on for both Spanish- and English-reading audiences.

Torment and Tequila in Belle Epoque Mexico

The Lottery Ticket

I.

Blas Carranza and Genoveva Villa would have enjoyed a perfect marriage if they had had everything the situation demanded. That included the means to pay the landlord, tailor, shoemaker, haberdasher, confectioner, and those many others who provided the services they needed. But as it was the couple were not happy, nor could they ever be so, for however hard they tried, they lacked the money to pay for those services. Hunger pains, the unclothed body, shoeless feet, or the insistent claims of creditors, from the butcher to the pharmacist, all demanded payment. None of these afflictions allow for that harmony and peace of mind that a happy union requires.

Blas was not without his gifts, but he could not develop them, partly because he lacked the money to do so, partly for his timid, even bashful, personality. True, quite a few millionaires, particularly those of the United States, have started out on the lowest rungs of society. We are talking about men like Cornelius Vanderbilt, who as an adolescent began as a boatman on the Hudson River, carrying grain to New York City. This did not stop him, and by dent of effort and persistence he eventually rose to become one of the world's leading capitalists. But it is also true that the brave souls who triumph in the end possess initiative and an open mind. The author Smiles proves this point in his book *Self-Help*, and the individuals he cites as examples of energy and resourcefulness in no way resemble Carranza.[1] Diminutive and diffident, he allowed the smallest setback to overcome him.

Despite everything Blas knew about agriculture, despite all his well-founded theories concerning irrigation and soil cultivation, and despite solidly grounded principles of animal husbandry—whether it be sheep, horses, cattle, or pigs—despite all this, he could never take advantage of his elevated knowledge. It redounded to his credit and edification but did little to overcome his hardships or the torments of hunger. The abrupt decline of his family resources had forced him to put aside his studies, and for that reason he never acquired a degree that might have given public guarantee of his professional abilities. But this was not why he had ended his scientific studies. He had once devoured books so insatiably that he memorized them from front to back or, better said, from one leather binding to the other. His love for agronomy and his wish to practice it had led him to acquire some half-broken flower pots; these he had filled with a few handfuls of dirt in which he planted, fertilized, and watered, and so conducted his experiments with different seeds, guano, and levels of moisture.[2] And with all the innocence of a child, he imagined that he was working vast haciendas and that what resulted would swell the granaries and his own pocket at the same time.

Anyone would have sworn that he was insane.

And so he passed his days, watering can in hand, removing soil, contemplating the mysteries of leveling, desiccation, cuttings, planting, dams, and stepping stones. All the while his better half wore herself out trying to put food on the table for them and their young son Lucianito, using nothing more than twenty or at most twenty-five centavos that the agronomist managed to earn on the side as a shopkeeper. Genoveva swept out their little apartment with those hands that resembled bunches of roses; she dusted off the walls and furniture, cleaned and polished the bricks and the glass, swept the floor, cooked the meals, and mended the clothes. She did everything slowly, mechanically, and with great care, so that even when it seemed she had not done so much, she kept everything in its place and ready for use. While she managed these chores, Lucianito toddled about with those slow steps of a child learning to walk. He managed to undo everything his mother had put in order. He hid under the chairs, tore up pieces of paper and scattered them on the floor, took vegetables from the basket, tipped over the stew pot, and got into any number of mischiefs and misdeeds. But throughout it all he never made his mother angry. Genoveva enjoyed herself amid all the uproar. All day long she shouted:

"Lucianito! Now look what you've done! Leave the candles alone! Careful with the newspapers! Don't put your hands in the water! Niño, niño, that's the shoe polish! You've turned into a little devil!"

Blas was physically present during these scenes, but in his mind he was far away, safely immersed in agrarian dreams. He had his occasional lucid moments, and at such times he lost himself in contemplating Genoveva, so young, so beautiful, so happy . . . and so unfortunate. It pained him to see her skirts turned into tatters, her shoes and stockings visible through the holes and the split fabric, her tiny feet white and blushing, delicate and shapely as those of a child. And there was her hair, so full that it resembled an imperial diadem, but tied in a simple Athenian knot over her head and adorned with stitched and discolored ribbons, because she had none of the silk or velvet bows that she so longed for. Painful too was the sight of Lucianito, who wore only coarse clothes, went around with his legs bare, and only wore shoes when outside the house.

In such moments Carranza sighed deeply and reflected with bitterness on what might lie at the root of these misfortunes. But when he found himself on the verge of tears or at the threshold of sheer desperation, he fell quickly and unconsciously into his accustomed reveries. He cast an ecstatic eye over vast meadows filled with herds of animals; he heard the roar of the bulls in the pasture, and the lowing of cows and calves in the stables; and he remained lost in contemplation of that deceptive mirage of abundant wheatfields, rows of succulent corn, echoing woods, streams of crystal-clear water, wagons laden with grain and produce, and the hustle and bustle of the great rural marketplace. Once his unbounded imagination was in play, it stopped for nothing. It had all the intensity of a shipwrecked sailor who sees mastheads, sails, smoke, and smokestacks on the sea's blank horizon, even as his own strength is giving out and he feels the rippling waves reaching his lips, filling his throat and lungs, and dragging him down to his death.

II.

Beside that same home where Carranza, Genoveva, and Lucianito resided, lived Don Ignacio and Damiana: father and sister of Genoveva, but also the curse and calamity of their in-laws. Don Ignacio was a clerk in the Ministry of Communications, and each month he brought in sixty hard-earned pesos. These were barely enough but more than sufficient to purchase for himself and his daughter an inexhaustible arrogance, enough to make them believe themselves heirs to a dynasty and to see Blas and his family as unfortunate and even inferior souls.

Don Ignacio was a bilious old man of sallow complexion. To hear him tell it, he did three times the work of any man. He crowed louder than the loudest rooster, and when he gave the order, the cannons fired, ready or not.

Damiana was an interminable chatterbox. She quarreled with the neighbors over the slightest cause, complained about the whole world, and told the morning star how to shine. She took particular exception to her sister's marriage. She talked endlessly about the wretchedness into which the house had fallen, of Blas's laziness, of Genoveva's lack of character. She called her sister a "slave," and an ugly one at that. Nor did she spare the ragged figure of Lucianito. Wicked tongues held that this old spinster, more freckled and yellowish than a turkey's egg, was frustrated about never having married and that to escape from her humiliation would even consent to marry the legless man who begged for alms at the door of the cathedral.[3] Whatever the truth in all of this, it is a fact that she obsessed about her sister's household and directed against it all her invective and disdain. Blood ties failed to touch her heart, nor did the profound poverty of those unfortunate relatives.

Our altogether true story opens on a splendid morning in early September. It had rained the night before, but the sky had cleared by daybreak and glowed with that deep blue of the rainy season.[4] Sunlight glistened in the water drops that clung to the window glass, and the heat pressing down from the sky caused a barely perceptible bluish vapor to rise from the wet thatch of the houses. Bird songs rang out from the cages adorning the walkways of the apartments, while impoverished girls of these dwellings, maidens now filled with a spirit of security and contentment, sang lines from the zarzuelas that were then popular.[5] Some of these songs dealt with love, others were bawdy, and still others sad, each reflecting the singer's mood. The morning was so radiant that it seemed a time to do away with prolonged stagnation, shake off entrenched sorrows, and shoulder long-postponed responsibilities. Marriageable girls hoped to make some brilliant conquest that day; ardent young men dreamed of dark-eyed nymphs and generous dowries . . . because today's gentlemen incline toward the positivist philosophy.[6]

Though an elderly man of gruff exterior, Don Ignacio himself was not immune to the influence of the bright sun and the newly refreshing air. It would be hard to explain how those soft breezes and that bright yellow sunlight might have loosened up and strengthened his wobbly limbs, his arthritic joints, or his worn-out tendons. But the fact was that the old man felt well indeed and spoke out with a voice that was stronger than ever, and each time his fist came down it made the objects on the table dance a sarabande.[7]

The fine weather had also produced nervous attacks, an acid tongue, and renewed bile in Damiana, who felt blessed in those moments, her tongue freer than ever, more creative, more gifted in invective. This has always been nature's way, giving one thing but taking away another, like the worm in the rose or the rattlesnake in the tropical garden. Life's exuberance places honeycombs in the cracks of rocks and poison in the mouths of reptiles.

Don Ignacio and Damiana had just eaten lunch and were conversing loudly at the table. Low and incessant, her voice resembled the sound of a fine rain, while his rang harsh and intermittent, like some thunderbolt let loose from the clouds.

"Father," said Damiana, "this situation is intolerable. I'm ashamed to live next door to these people. They're at God's mercy and good for nothing. When people see a boy as ragged as Lucianito or someone as weak as Genoveva, they're going to suppose that we're like them: that I'm your servant and you're one of the seven sleepers, some groundhog that never wakes up."[8]

"I'll knock the daylights out of the first person who says it," the old secretary roared out.

"I doubt they'll say it to your face. They say that sort of thing on the sly because they know you have your dignity and that you tolerate no slights. But they think it and whisper it among themselves. I'm beside myself when I think that the neighbors see us that way, that they're watching us when we go by, that they're nudging each other in our very presence."

"Who are they?" Don Ignacio exclaimed, even more choleric than usual. "Tell me who they are!"

"The whole world, Father. Don't get excited. You can't possibly shut every mouth everywhere. And it also occurs to me that they're going to criticize us for not maintaining these three beggars as much as we should. They must be saying that we're selfish, that we're lazy and ill-intentioned. As if we were obliged to dress in rags to clothe them, or as if it were somehow a virtue to foster lazy relatives."

"Blas is a complete layabout," Don Ignacio complained.

"He has no refinement," Damiana added. "He spends the whole day tending plants and watering flowerpots, like some love-sick girl, and lets the world go on as if he didn't have a wife and son. It's lucky for Blas that he took up with a woman who doesn't look like your daughter or my sister,[9] someone with no self-respect, and no way to make someone respect her. She's on bended knees, and is cook, washerwoman, seamstress, chambermaid, errand girl, and slave, all at the same time."

"I don't know how she puts up with all that," Don Ignacio exclaimed as he clinched his fists. "I should have taught them a lesson a long time ago."

"And they deserve it, Father, for I've never seen anything like this in my life. Even though the people around us are our inferiors, they're still a cut above these relatives of ours. The tinsmith in front of us has regular work and keeps a seven-year-old girl to help his wife. The tailor in the second patio over always gives his wife four reales[10] every day, and if he doesn't, she gives him nothing to eat. Meanwhile, Blas isn't making more than a few centavos each day, never as much as thirty, and he expects his wife to work miracles with that, to handle all the responsibilities of the house!"

Don Ignacio was livid.

"In reality, Father, although it hurts to confess it, Blas is worth less than the tinsmith and doesn't even measure up to the tailor. He ought to be kissing the feet of the cart man. And as for the way he treats Genoveva, she's like a woman's worn-out old shoe . . . a woman of some real man, that is, not of Carranza."

The old man snorted. His daughter's words slowly began to burn, until he fell into a fit like some raging bull. He tried to get up but was unable to do so, for his legs trembled and he felt dizzy.

"I'm going to give that son-in-law a beating this very instant," he growled between clenched teeth. "If he's that given to staying at home, I'll make sure he has good reason to lie in bed. He doesn't know who he's dealing with."

"No, Father, nothing of the sort." Damiana objected, for she realized that her words had gone too far. "Not that, because it's going to cause an even greater scandal."

"What do I care?"

"Our position, Father, for the love of God, we have to protect our position."

This argument proved incontrovertible. Don Ignacio realized that being who he was, and his own daughter being the woman of the house in question, and taking into account that they all lived in the same plebeian neighborhood, then it was not so good an idea to speak out of turn, much less to have the police intervene and carry them all off to the station.

"But then what should I do?" sighed the put-upon old man. "On one hand, you get me all worked up; and on the other, you forbid me from taking action."

"It's clear that we have to do something. But it has to help the situation, not make it worse."

"Like what, for example?"

"Force Blas to get a job."

"It would be easier to make Iztaccíhuatl get up and walk."[11]

"No one can stand up to you, much less a spineless individual like him."

"So you think I can do it?"

"I'm certain of it."

"You may well be right. If that's the case, I've got to get started immediately. I've got to put a fire under that deadbeat before I go to work."

And since Don Ignacio was an impulsive man, he rose from his chair as though propelled upward by a spring. He took his hat from its peg, along with the heavy oak walking cane (which he had baptized with the descriptive name of "Lunatic Tamer") from a corner of the room, and in two or three strides to the door of the adjoining quarters, into which he rushed without so much as a word.

III.

Blas had just gone out of his hovel at that moment, carrying an old watering can that he used to freshen the roots of his precious vegetables. It was at that precise moment that Don Ignacio burst into the patio like a gust of wind, violently striking the pavement with his cane at each step he took. The dilettante agronomist stood with his mouth open, motionless before the presence of his august father-in-law. He held the watering can high, half-tilted toward the flowerpots, but in his surprise he aimed poorly. The water dribbled out of the can, arched in a useless parabola, and fell like lead onto his dingy, worn-out shoes.

"Good morning," the old man exclaimed fiercely.

"Good morning, Señor Don Ignacio," the young man replied warily.

"Where is my daughter?"

"Getting the baby dressed and cleaned."

"And you, what are you doing?"

"As always, I'm conducting experiments."

"Experiments of what sort?"

"Agricultural experiments, señor."

"I would say that you are amusing yourself and wasting your time. What good is that nonsense to you and your family? It would be far more beneficial if you were to saw lumber or make adobe bricks. At least you'd earn a day's wage, and my daughter and grandson would have some relief."

"But if I manage to get a plot of land, that is, if God grants me that. . . ."

"You'll cultivate it keeping with the rules of agronomy. Isn't that right?" At this point Don Ignacio burst out into an ironic guffaw almost like a roar. "And when will that be? Sometime in the next century? There's no reason to think that it could happen sooner. But you're capable of pinching an ox to death or planting one of those trees that only bears fruit after a hundred years. But you're lazy enough to make the Aztec calendar angry."[12]

And so saying, the old man took out Lunatic Tamer and let it fall squarely on the flower pots. With a loud crash they shattered to pieces, covering the tiles with broken crockery and rich, black soil. The shoots of the tender plants that the agronomist had tended with such care lay crushed and broken by the fall. The soil removed, the precious and delicate roots were exposed, some long and fine like a woman's hair, others thick and bulbous like the domes and towers of Moscow.[13]

The blood suddenly rushed to Blas's face. The brutal event had wounded both his dignity and his passions, and he moved to throw the watering can at his father-in-law's face. At that very moment Genoveva appeared in a hurry, frightened, uncombed, and still wearing the papers she used to crinkle her hair.

"What is this? What's happening?" she asked, thoroughly alarmed.

"The problem is your husband, who wanted to throw that watering can at my head!" the old man exclaimed.

"The problem is you, Father-in-law, who broke my flowerpots!" Blas let out, sobbing. "But why?"

"And you ask me?" Don Ignacio answered. "You should know better than I. Because this phlegmatic loafer is making my blood boil! He barely moves, he doesn't work, he does nothing useful. He wastes his time watering plants."

"And so what, Father?"

"It's that I can't put up with it anymore, that it needs to stop, and I'm determined to make it stop."

"And that's why you did . . . what you did?" Genoveva retorted, scarcely containing her anger.

"Yes, because of that. Understand? Because of that. Does it strike you as wrong?"

"No, father, but . . ."

"No buts about it! I need to put this house in order, even if it means breaking the bones of everyone who lives here. You'll see how I motivate them: even turtles move when there's a fire."

"Señor," Blas stammered, his gusto now gone and his habitual timidity returned. "You know perfectly well that I'm eager to work."

"No, I don't know that. Don't insult my intelligence."

"Yes, señor. What happens is that I have no one to help me, and no resources of my own."

"To a capable man the four natural elements are enough: water, earth, fire, and air. But what you're lacking is shame."

"Father, for the love of God," Genoveva interrupted with tears in her eyes. "We haven't injured you in any way, neither asking favor nor complaining."

"Do you think I'm made of stone? Who could see this scene without feeling enraged?"

Once more excited, Blas thought of telling his father-in-law, "Well, don't look at it." But Genoveva read his intentions and headed him off by saying:

"Neither my son nor I are complaining. Everyone's happy."

"So you cry, eh? But that's because you and my grandson have the souls of slaves, just like Damiana says."

"Father," Genoveva moaned, "I can scarcely believe that you are coming here to add to our problems!"

"It's because I'm a monster. But later you're going to thank me." Then, directing himself to Blas, he continued: "Hey! Put on a jacket, grab your hat, and follow me!"

"Where are you taking him?" Genoveva asked.

"To work!" shouted Don Ignacio.

Intimidated yet again, Blas obeyed without a word. Thereupon Don Ignacio shot through the door like an arrow. The young woman embraced her husband and said: "Forgive him, Blas, he's my father. Come back as soon as possible."

By way of answer, the agronomist kissed Genoveva on the forehead and went off with his father-in-law.

IV.

An hour had not passed when Blas returned home, sadder and more dejected than ever.

"Why have you come back so downcast?" his wife asked. "Did something happen?"

"Yes," Blas replied. "I don't have my watch anymore."

"Did someone steal it?" the young woman asked, now visibly pale.

"No. I'm going to lose it because of Don Ignacio."

So saying, the poor man threw himself down into a chair, placed his head in his hands, and wept like a little child. That watch, its mounting, its chimes, and its gold case were all that he had received from his father. He valued it greatly and even in the greatest depths of his misery had never dreamed of selling it. He had often told his wife that he wanted to be buried with it.

"But why do you say that it was because of my father?" Genoveva delicately inquired, gently peeling his hands away from his face. "Why do you say this?"

"Because he has it," the young man answered with irritation. "Because it's impossible to get the watch back from where it is now."

"You pawned it?"

"Yes, for twenty pesos."

"That's nothing. You can get it back any time."

"No, no," murmured Blas as he shook his head disconsolately. "I'll never get together enough money to get it out of the pawnshop. The time limit for the ticket is going to run out, and I'll lose it."

Genoveva realized that her husband was right. And because there was nothing she could say to cheer him up, she tried to distract him by changing the subject with a different line of questions.

"How did this happen? You haven't told me. Did Father want you to come up with money for our expenses?"

"It wasn't that. He tried to get money for work, a fund to get me started."

"So now you come home rich," said Genoveva, trying to put a good face on things. "Well, Mr. Money!"

Her rosy fingers tapped with loving confidence against the pockets of Blas's vest. But to her surprise, she felt no money there.

"What money?" moaned Carranza. "That's the saddest part. I'm coming home as poor as when I left, without a cent in my pocket."

Genoveva's eyes opened wide.

"But then how did that happen?"

"My twenty pesos have turned into paper," Blas answered indignantly. As he did so he took a lottery ticket out of his pocket.

The young woman stood petrified. To spend twenty pesos on a lottery ticket when there was no charcoal in the kitchen and when they were short on everything, from their clothes to their shoes, he, she, and the child! From the expression on her face, he knew what she was thinking.

"But blessed wife, do you really think that I'm capable of such madness?"

"Who, then?"

"Your father, Don Ignacio, my father-in-law . . ."

"How could this be?"

"It's very simple. We left the house without saying a word, and both keeping our distance. He walked ahead, very quickly, and I followed him as well as I could. Pretty soon we passed the pawnshop of that Spaniard, Don Quintín, that's on the corner. Don Ignacio stopped and asked me if I had brought my watch. I told him I had, and he demanded that I give it to him. As soon as he had it in his hands he went into the pawnshop and handed it over to the Spaniard and asked how much he would give for it. While the Spaniard was looking it over, I asked Don Ignacio what this was all about, and he told me that it was ridiculous for me to carry around a precious thing like that when there was nothing to eat in my house and that I needed to pawn it to get enough money to manage on.

"But I objected. I told him that it was the only thing of value that remained from my father, that I loved it dearly, and that I in no way wanted to risk losing it. He growled, and the pawn dealer said that he could give sixty pesos for it, and your father agreed. But I was put out, and refused to consent to such an expensive transaction, because I realized that the greater the amount the pawnbroker gave, the harder it would be for me to redeem the watch. Your father insisted on the idea, the pawnbroker declared that since I was the watch's owner, he wouldn't give so much as a centavo without my consent. By now your father was furious but gradually began to lower his demands. All the while I kept refusing. So, the amount went from fifty pesos to forty, and then from forty to thirty. When it got to twenty pesos, I no longer had the power to resist, for I was afraid that he was going to hit me right then and there.

"Don Ignacio collected the money and handed me the ticket when we left the shop. All the way he kept at me for not accepting more money; he said that with a trifling amount of money like that it wasn't possible to start anything, and that the most I could do with it was throw it in the trash. Meanwhile, I was thinking that with things as they were, I didn't see why we had pawned the watch—and that if the twenty pesos were worthless, then the sensible thing to do would be to return them to the pawnbroker. I tried to suggest this as gently as possible. But when he shot me an angry glance, I said nothing, and we kept on walking.

"But it so happened that we passed in front of a tobacco shop. We stopped there for a moment, and he told me that he had a brilliant idea: invest my money in the $100,000 peso lottery drawing that was being held today; that if luck was on my side, it would make me rich immediately. Your father also added that he had brought along the money to buy himself a ticket as well. Without further remarks he took the money and went into the shop while I stayed outside. A few minutes later he came out with two tickets in hand; their numbers were 3,312 and 777. It took him a while to decide which one to give me, but he eventually settled on 3,312. With that out of the way, he said goodbye, sarcastically telling me to go home and tend my vegetables and my flowerpots while I was waiting to see what luck would bring. And here I am, Genoveva," Carranza concluded, "without the watch, without the money, and with this flimsy, useless piece of paper, the only reward for everything I've suffered."

"Good heavens!" the young woman said with evident pain. "And to think of all the things we could have done with those twenty pesos!"

"That's what I say. At the very least, we could have gotten past some of the problems with the money from my father's watch."

"I have no faith in the lottery," Genoveva continued as she unfolded the piece of paper.

"Me, neither," her husband added. "So far I've never seen anyone win it; and I know a lot of poor people who've sacrificed their whole lives to buy those infernal tickets. . . ."

"May God's will be done," his wife concluded in resignation. She folded up the paper again and tucked it away in his pocket. "Watch and money both lost!"

V.

Blas and Genoveva were eating when the door opened with a bang and in came Damiana. It never even occurred to her to say hello. She went straight over to the young man and said:

"Why are you doing such things to my father?"

"What things?" the confused young man asked.

"Things like this," the harpy replied, holding out the other ticket in her hand.

"That?" Carranza replied without really understanding what he was saying.

"Yes! This! This!" the spinster shouted, almost sticking the paper into his nose. "It seems that you don't so much as break a plate, but you water your flowerpots; you don't work, but when you're able you take advantage of respectable folk."

"Why don't you talk sense?" Genoveva interrupted indignantly. "What right do you have to treat my husband this way?"

"It's my right to defend my father . . . *your* father," she said, directing her words to her sister, "however much you dislike the idea."

"Don Ignacio doesn't need someone to defend him," Carranza objected. "What are you complaining about? Didn't he do whatever he wanted with me? Didn't he force me to pawn my watch?"

"And it's good that he did. You ought to have pawned that watch years ago. And you kindly took revenge for the favor he did you."

"How's that?" the astonished young man asked.

"By taking the ticket with the better number for yourself."

"A lie!" Blas replied, now exasperated. "He took the one he wanted. He's the one who decided."

The spinster shot back, "Supposing that you agreed to that without a word and were only too happy to take what he offered . . ."

"All I did was obey."

"Go ahead, you deadbeat, deceive whomever you can with your tricks. Maybe that simpleton," she said, directing herself once more to Genoveva, "but not me."

"That's enough," Genoveva cut in, irritated. "What did you come here for? To insult us? What do you want?"

"All I want is for Blas to do the decent thing and give me the ticket he's got, and that he take this one. The number 777 is terrible because it has three 7's, and seven is the number of the seven deadly sins."

"But that means that you're trying to give us the worst number," said Genoveva.

"I'm trying to undo an injustice."

"To commit one, you mean to say," Genoveva replied.

"However you want to look at it," the sister replied. "What matters is that you give me the other ticket."

"And if we don't?"

"Even the deaf are going to hear about it!"

"Let 'em hear you."

"Come on, Blas," Damiana shouted imperiously, "hand over the other ticket."

"Hija," Carranza murmured to his wife, "give it to her. It's for the best."

Genoveva was so submissive that quickly enough she took out the ticket. But irritated by the injustice, she kept it in her hand and said:

"No. Why do we have to let you play with us this way? Because we're poor?"

"The ticket right now!" Damiana ordered.

"No!"

"Yes!"

"Not now, not ever!"

"We'll see about that!"

"We'll see!"

Quicker than can be imagined, and before Genoveva could stop her, Damiana snatched away the ticket that her sister was holding in her right hand and let fall the ticket with the number 777 and went running away to her room. Genoveva followed after her just as quickly but couldn't stop her before she entered her home.

She stopped perplexed before the closed door. Despite her disgust, she thought for a moment about what could happen if Don Ignacio were to intervene in the matter: screaming, uproar, even blows, and then the police, and the scandal. For that reason, she limited herself to shouting through the keyhole:

"You're unjust and wicked, Damiana. You have no pity for us. But God will judge you."

And she went back to her home in tears. When she entered she picked up the number 777 that had remained on the floor and to her husband expressed her rage about what had happened.

Blas became furious and said that things could not go on like this. But little by little he calmed down and also managed to reassure Genoveva as well, saying: "Don't worry, and don't torture yourself. Neither one of these numbers is going to win the lottery."

VI.

In the afternoon of the following day Carranza was busy transferring as best he could the soil and the plants from his old planters to some pots and clay bowls from the kitchen, when Genoveva interrupted him.

"And the lottery ticket?" she asked.

"What about it?" Blas responded indifferently.

"It's time to check it. They held the drawing yesterday and the results should be posted already."

"It's no use, *hija*, we didn't win anything."

"But now that it's all we have left, thanks to Damiana, it's important to check. Maybe God's going to punish her and that the number she rejected is going to win."

"Hmph!" said Blas skeptically. "Then you handle it. I'm busy."

"Alright. The tobacco shop isn't far away, and the list of winners should be posted on the door. It will also give me the chance to say hello to Conchita. I haven't seen her for ages."

Blas did not hear his wife's final remarks, for he was already lost in the process of propping up his plants' broken stalks with a stick.

Genoveva threw on her mantle, and without bothering to check herself in the mirror as she would surely have done, given her youth and beauty, she left Lucianito happily tearing up paper.

When she opened the door she saw that at that moment Damiana was returning home with a feathered hat, gloves, parasol, and everything else needed for bad weather; she hurriedly entered her home and slammed the door shut. Genoveva waited for a few moments then slipped quietly, almost furtively, through the passageway.

In the distance she could see the lottery results posted on the door of the tobacco shop, printed on a large, unfolded sheet of paper and in large letters, as was the practice with this sort of high-stakes drawing.

"My God," she silently and humbly prayed. "Let us win fifty pesos. I don't ask for more than fifty. You know only too well how needy we are, and how this special help would make us very happy. In reality, Señor, it doesn't have to be more than thirty, because the ticket cost twenty."

But deep in her heart, timidly, secretly, she nursed hopes of better fortune.

Before arriving she had time to build castles in the air. First, if God were to hear her prayers, she would redeem Carranza's watch. She would then buy two sets of clothes for Lucianito, a cap, some slippers, and two pairs of stockings. Finally, she would replace her husband's shoes and some of the plants that Don Ignacio had destroyed. It never occurred to her to buy anything for herself, even though she was lacking in all regards. In this way she reached her destination, lost in her humble monologue.

"Good afternoon, Conchita," she said as she reached the counter and extended a hand to the matron of the establishment.

"Good afternoon, Genoveva," the old woman answered, receiving and caressing her visitor's soft, white, and unhealthy hand. Conchita was an old woman with gray hair, widow of one of the captains of Santa Anna.[14] She was good-tempered, tidy, and quite the conversationalist. Her late husband had left her impoverished, and she made a living selling liquor, matches, all sorts of stamps, and lottery tickets in a place so small that it was no wider or taller than a door. She was friendly by nature, but more curious and long-winded than most. Genoveva knew her well and arrived ready for anything.

"Where did the sun go?" asked the old woman.

"Why do you say that, Conchita?" asked the young woman, her smile revealing her fine white teeth.

"Because you're showing your face, Geno. It's been a long time since you've come around here."

"Lucianito doesn't leave me time to go out."

"And there's your situation, isn't there? I know that Don Blas doesn't earn much."

"No, Conchita," the young woman replied with self-assurance, "the truth is that we're not doing so badly. Lately we've had a few lucky breaks, thank God. We're even thinking of moving from where we live; but we haven't done so to avoid living apart from my father."

"People, niña, how they gossip. May you live for many years and may you prosper."

"May God reward you, Conchita. Now I've come to check the list for the 100,000-peso prize. We took a chance on a 20-peso ticket."

"There it is on your right, Geno. They just brought it."

Turning her head, the young woman cast her eyes on the center of the paper, and there, in enormous characters, in a huge space adorned with thick lines resembling the rays of the sun, she beheld the number of the prize-winning ticket:

3,312

Emotion overpowered her. Her ears buzzed, blood pounded through her heart, and she nearly fainted.

Don Blas's ticket, their ticket, the ticket that Damiana had taken by force: it had won the 100,000-peso prize!

She, Blas, and Lucianito had held it in their hands, and it had been stolen from them. And now her dark misery, a misery that admitted no hope, seemed more horrible than ever.

"Jesús! Jesús!" Conchita exclaimed, surprised, as she leaned over the counter to try to help. "Geno, Geno! What's the matter?"

"It's nothing," Genoveva answered as she struggled to compose herself. "It's just that I'm overcome by the emotion of having held number 3,312 in my hands. And if I had kept it, I would have escaped this poverty."

"What doesn't happen, *mi alma,* what doesn't happen. . . . But who took it from you? Have you checked your ticket?"

"Not yet, Conchita. I was so overcome that I forgot."

"Let's see, give it to me, Geno, and I'll check . . . 777 . . . let's have a look at the 700s . . . 710 . . . 725 . . . 7761! You almost won ten pesos. But your number didn't come up. Let's check the nearby winner . . . no, there's nothing there. What a shame, Geno, I'm so sorry."

And so saying, Conchita returned the transparently thin and useless slip of paper. Genoveva took it without looking and mechanically placed it in her pocket as she prepared to leave.

Conchita was pained to see her so disconsolate, and she stopped her for a moment.

"It's true that you didn't win anything, but at the same time, I think I have some good news for you."

"What?" Genoveva asked, barely knowing what to say.

"That your sister Damiana won a major prize."

"Oh!" responded Genoveva, barely fending off another fainting spell.

"Yes," the shop woman continued, thinking that her friend's emotion was one of joy. "But calm yourself. Why are you so nervous, niña? Could it be that the stork is bringing you another baby?"[15]

Genoveva shook her head no.

"Well, that's strange," Conchita rambled on, "because you look absolutely startled, and anyone would think. . . . Well, the truth is that Damiana just left here as pleased as could be. I don't know how much she won, because she wouldn't show me her ticket, even when it was there in her hand. She's so surprised! Before coming she even memorized the number by heart so that no one could see it. But the prize must have been pretty good, because her face turned red, and her eyes sparkled. However much she tried to conceal her excitement, she couldn't do it. When I asked her about the good news, she tried to deny it, but eventually she had to confess the truth. She told me that she had won five hundred pesos, and she offered to give me five. And so, Geno, things aren't going so badly for your family because you, your father, and your sister are the same person. What belongs to one belongs to everyone. That's the way it works in unified families like yours."

Those words fell like daggers in the young woman's heart. She grimaced, and with tears in her eyes, quickly walked out of the shop.

"You're right, Conchita," she murmured as she left, "you're right."

When she got home she began to cry out loud.

"We didn't win anything?" Blas asked.

"Nothing."

"I told you so. But don't cry, woman. Did you really think we were going to win the grand prize?"

"I'm not crying about that," Genoveva replied while sobbing loudly, "but because this very day we were about to escape from poverty. God had decided it."

"I don't understand."

"The number that won the grand prize of 100,000 pesos was 3,312—your number, the same one that Damiana took away from me."

"What! Is this true?" a livid Blas demanded.

"True, completely true. Go ahead, check the list, go see for yourself."

For the first time in his life Carranza felt his nerves shaking from profound indignation. He shouted that they had been robbed, that it was intolerable, that he would take the matter to court, and that if the magistrate did nothing, then he would set the world on fire. But after this explosion he gradually sank back into the apathy of the powerless, only deeper than ever, because he realized that his poverty did not allow him to pay for attorneys or shoulder any of the costs associated with a lawsuit. And above all, he had no proof of any crime.

"What hurts me the most," he said at last with a debilitated voice, "is losing my father's watch. They'll sell it off in the pawnshop. I'll never see it again."

And rubbing his eyes with his clenched fist he sang a duet of sorrow with Genoveva, like an overgrown child.

VII.

So it was that the two families followed different paths. For Don Ignacio, thrifty and a good administrator with a head for business, knew how to get the most out of those hundred thousand pesos. He converted them into an immense fortune, one that allowed him to rub shoulders with famous investors in the capital. He now has a beautiful mansion on the Avenida de la Reforma and rides through Chapultepec

Park in a luxurious Landau carriage with liveried servants.[16] Damiana rides beside him. She is old and ugly but elegant, her hands gloved and her faced protected from the sun by expensive parasols adorned with light-colored Chantilly lace.

Meanwhile, Blas, Genoveva, and their young child have sunk further down the rungs of misery, at last reaching the lowest, saddest, and gloomiest of positions. Nothing further is known of them. In their tragic journey they ended up losing themselves in the darkness, unable to resolve problems, be they trivial or complicated, of lodging, food, and clothing. Only God knows whether they are already dead, or whether they have taken refuge in some shelter of charity, or whether they go from door to door collecting rags and crusts of bread.

The Mirror

I.

Miguel Villena's dedication to the world of letters had awakened in his soul the love of ideals: for him the ground on which he trod was nothing but a pedestal for his dreams. His thoughts inhabited a world quite different from that which lay here beneath the moon, the world where he lived and breathed.[1] The echoes of social life reached him in weak and confused form, like the vague sound of some faraway river. Thanks to his exquisite sensibility his spirit continually suffered violent agitations: he was unable to rest, for he suffered inordinately from afflictions both great and small.

While scarcely a young man, he met a lass who deeply stirred his emotions, and who from the very beginning was the sum of his dreams, the embodiment of his hopes, and the fulfillment of all his vows. Her name was Aurora, and she combined all the elements of beauty that are the stuff of dreams. Her skin was white and pearl-like, like some elaborate vase wreathed with roses. Her eyes were blue like the diaphanous space through which one beholds the heavens. The thick, blonde tresses that covered her head formed a golden diadem for her queenly forehead. The sound of her childlike voice made him swoon in ecstasy whenever he heard it. Much the same was her laugh, like the murmuring of a fountain, and her white slender hands called to mind those of ancient statues. Her rhythmic steps seemed guided by some inner cadence. Everything about her was light, harmony, and beauty.

Faced with Miguel's impetuous passions, she fell subjugated like a slave before her master. And as a hurricane carries off tiny bits of chaff, Miguel's love swept away Aurora's heart. The couple were deeply in love, and they long awaited the day of supreme happiness. At last came the moment they had so impatiently longed for, and their destinies were united forever.

From that moment they began a life of ecstasy. When each was beside the other, they felt as joyful as if they possessed all the treasures of the earth. Wrapped in their love they saw nothing outside of it. People, society, ambition, pride, all of them forces that troubled whatever they touched: for this couple they were nothing more than a confused whirlwind that could not take them out of their bliss. Hand in hand, they gazed into each other's souls and pledged eternal love, the words enraptured them, and on the wings of illusion they ascended into the heaven of infinite happiness.

What master of the canvas could paint the ineffable joys of a pure and immense love when it carries away the dreaming souls who join together and become one, without bashfulness or remorse before either heaven or earth? Tender glances, soft smiles, languid sighs, affectionate words, chaste kisses: and all these things are notes of that celestial hymn called love, the song of the blissful souls of this life, like a prelude to that of the immortal voices that resound on high.

II.

The Lord blessed this couple's love by sending them a son as beautiful as the lovers themselves. The infant resembled one of those angels surrounding the Virgin of Murillo.[2] And the couple continued in love after the child was born. He was a separate being for them and yet a part of them as well: their love in human form, a point of convergence of the two lives. To feel themselves both reproduced, reborn in life, to see themselves blended together as a single being: what happiness! They gazed at the child like a mirror of themselves, and they adored him because they adored one another. They spent hours contemplating him. They went out of their minds with joy on seeing him smile and move his pink hands; they revered his smiling face with kisses when, upon opening his eyes, he trilled like a songbird.

It would be impossible to number the plans they made for this budding life. They could already see their child growing, always beautiful, enlivening the house with his infant games. He was intelligent, good-hearted, and affectionate. All other parents envied him. What enormous dedication they would devote to him! To care for him like their only treasure, omitting no sacrifice; if necessary, the blood in their veins would strengthen him, and their own breasts would form a shield around hm.

Anxiously they waited for him to say his first word. Would it be *papá* or *mamá*? It was a problem that worried them deeply. Enchanting child! He could not have been more beautiful, being the fruit of a love so grand and so pure.

III.

But destiny casts an evil eye on those who are happy. It is jealous, and good fortune deepens that jealousy. As a wild beast spies on its prey, so Fortune looks at those with heaven in their hearts and waits for the moment to wound them in the cruelest possible manner. When have we seen a happiness that did not turn tragic? Through the smile, in moments of the sweetest joy, we can see glistening tears. The human being is predestined to sorrow, as a victim is destined for sacrifice. Happiness is but the splendid surface of sorrow, like the glimmer of the ocean as it reflects the sky, but which only serves to conceal the abyss below.

Suddenly, and for causes unknown, Aurora's health failed. Her dazzling beauty began to suffer. Her cheeks grew pale, like flowers deprived of sunlight; the gleam in her eyes was extinguished, like stars obscured by some dense cloud; her red lips lost their color, like fading carnations; her weak and trembling voice sounded like a whisper.

Miguel's heart shattered before so painful a sight. He did not understand how an existence that was so intimately linked to his own could somehow separate itself; how the joy that had taken so deep a root in his heart could be torn out. Nor did he understand how his own life could go on without that point of light and harmony from which his heart drew warmth and dreams. And like a shipwrecked sailor who makes a supreme effort not to drown, he struggled to cling to that existence that was escaping him like water bursting through a dike.

Horrified, Aurora could not bear the idea of dying. What? To die in the very flower of youth, when she had an affectionate and beloved husband and a beautiful child and felt her own heart filled with happiness! Before this notion her heart froze in terror; she cried out to Miguel and, taking his hands and covering them with kisses and tears, she said: "Miguel! Miguel! I don't want to die, don't let me die!"

Upon hearing these words, the young men felt as if his heart were breaking, like a lyre whose strings were too tight, and he cried like a madman. He searched his mind for some way to save his beloved Aurora, and he answered her with powerful sobs: "You can't die. How can you die without me dying?"

His mind convulsed by suffering, he consequently began to entertain certain dark notions; for he thought it was necessary for both to die at the same time, or else for neither to die. So tightly entwined were their two lives!

But all the while the cruel disease continued its tragic course. At last Aurora realized that she could not go on living, and although her soul was shattered, she resigned herself in a sweet and Christian manner to receive the blow unleashed by the hand of God. And in place of the agitation in which she had found herself came a bitter calm that made her resemble a martyr soon to receive the palm of triumph from the hands of angels.

But two things continued to trouble her: her child's future and her husband's happiness. When from time to time it occurred to her that Miguel could love again, that he could give his heart to another woman, then Aurora felt that she lacked the strength for such a sacrifice. Such thoughts condemned her to die in desperation. Already she imagined seeing her tender son, the child of her womb, in the clutches of a harsh and jealous stepmother. She could see the boy filthy and ill-clad, hiding forgotten in the corners of the house, a homeless orphan, now thin and pale, inspiring pity among the neighbors and crying for his mother's memory!

She felt her reason unraveling before such heart-rending scenes. She wanted Miguel to love no other person again, ever. Let him live with her memory as he had lived with her love! It was only just; anything else would be a crime.

The husband watched in sorrow as these worries etched themselves upon Aurora's brow, like storm clouds covering the sky. But in vain he asked her of the cause of her grief, for she stubbornly refused to reveal it.

And so things went on until one day, when the dizziness born of pain reached its height and very nearly overcame her. She broke her obstinate silence and burst into sobs. The inner struggle that had continued for so many days had worn away her scant strength. Her altered expression and the paleness and transparency of her skin gave her the appearance of someone who had been raised from the dead. There was a strange look in her eye, and her weak voice sounded like some subterranean echo. Her soul teetered on the boundary between this world and the next, simultaneously illuminated by light from both. An august solemnity surrounded her.

In that supreme moment she called her husband to her side and in a short, labored voice, and with the look of death in her eyes, she said: "Miguel, I feel my life slipping away. In a few brief moments I will cease to exist."

"Don't say that!" Miguel replied with broken voice. "You won't die. You will live for my affection, for my happiness."

"Ah! Impossible!" said the stricken woman, raising her pallid hand and running it through her husband's hair. "I have asked God for much, but He did not wish to give it to me. May His holy will be done! There's no point in thinking any more about it. Let us talk about something important, and we have to resolve it before I die, so that my death can be peaceful! Tell me, after I have left this world, will you love again?"

And so saying, she threw back the locks of her hair that had fallen over her husband's brow, and holding his head firm, forced him to raise his glance and look her in the face.

"Aurora," Miguel answered with a tone of reproach, "how dare you ask me that question? You know I adore you, and that my soul, my life, and my very being belong to you. To you alone. To you alone, now and forever!"

"You're too young," Aurora answered bitterly, "and very impetuous, a dreamer. Your illusions will return all too soon. All the love that I have for you (God knows that it is enormous) will become nothing more than an episode in your life. With the passing of time, you will soon forget the tragedy you are about to witness."

"I will never forget it, my Aurora: your words tear into my heart."

"If only I could believe it, my last wish would be to bless you. The fate of this poor child, our son, fills me with sorrow. What will become of him if you give him a stepmother?"

"For the love of God, don't say such things. You're hurting the both of us, Aurora."

"Do you want me to die in peace?"

"I would spare no sacrifice to calm your spirit."

"Then swear on this crucifix that you will have no other woman, and that you will not place my son in the hands of a stepmother."

Miguel took the holy object and without hesitating said: "I swear by this holy crucifix that I will love no other woman after you, and that I will not give a stepmother to my son."

Upon hearing this a faint gleam of happiness shown in Aurora's exhausted eyes.

"And I pledge to you," she said, speaking like an *alumbrada*[3] and forming her words with effort, "that if you fail in that promise, I will return to punish your perjury."

"I accept that," her husband solemnly promised.

"May God reward you," Aurora added with a scarcely perceptible voice. "I will take my leave peaceful and contented."

She searched for Miguel's hand and taking it with her own icy fingers placed it over her faintly beating heart. A few moments passed in this fashion. Afterward she opened her eyes as though in fright and cried: "My son! My son! I want to see my son!"

Her order was instantly obeyed. She stretched out her trembling hand and gave the child a final caress. Then she asked for the crucifix and taking it fixed her glassy eyes upon it.

At that moment the priest entered. Aurora had already received last rites, and her soul was as clear as that of a child. With a long, blessed candle in one hand and a devotional text in the other, the priest began to pray with visible emotion. Meanwhile, Miguel smothered his sobbing as he knelt and fixed his tear-filled eyes on the dying woman's face.

Aurora was slipping away little by little. Her breath became labored and wheezing. Her chest rose mechanically, only to falter with time. An ill-defined shadow came over her face, as if some invisible hand had cast a dark, thin veil upon it. Her eyes took on a strange, fixed grace. They grew clouded, and her lips moved sweetly, as if in prayer.

Slowly and with immense effort she raised the hand that held the crucifix and brought it to her lips to kiss the divine feet of the Savior.

At that point the priest said with a clear voice: "May a shining squadron of angels receive you; and the chorus of the patriarchs, the apostles, and the Virgin receive you in its bosom, raising you to the world of eternal rest!"

The words of this prayer still echoed when Aurora had already flown to join with the heavenly chorus the priest had invoked. He ceased to speak and those who knelt around him grew silent as well. Only Miguel broke the silence of the solemn gathering.

"It can't be! It can't be!" he cried. "She's not dead, I'm sure she's not dead!"

And approaching Aurora, he touched her forehead and hands with feverish anguish and sought in vain for a heartbeat, kissing the cadaver with his sobbing lips he seemed to infuse it with his own breath.

IV.

The afflicted husband lost all reason with the force of that terrible blow. Frantically entangled with Aurora's cadaver, he was like a shipwrecked sailor clutching some fragile board that offered his only hope. The sobs and sighs that issued from his chest broke the hearts of those around him. It was the voice of profound, intimate pain, one of those sounds that issue from individuals of a special nature, and that agitate all the powers of the body and the faculties of the spirit. That fury, surpassing the bounds of common suffering, assumed the characteristics of a mortal crisis, turning Miguel into a sick and unhinged being. For pity's sake it was necessary to separate him from the dead woman. His friends assumed responsibility for this; they feared that the young widower's reason might suffer permanent damage.

They led him into the adjoining room and laid him down on the bed, using gentle and persuasive words to lull him into a prudent calm, and doctors intervened to administer a sedative that soothed his convulsions.

After the initial fury, during which moments Miguel rabidly hurled insults at his friends, calling them *cruel*, *executioners*, and *traitors*, his cataract-like eyes opened and let loose rivers of tears that bathed his face like a benevolent dew.

That catharsis, which lasted for several hours, was followed by a deep depression. Next came lethargy, the weighty and painful lethargy that, more than rest, was better called collapse, a weakening of life, a loss of energy, an exhaustion of any power to endure the torture. During this period the young man lost awareness of events but retained that dim perception of pain, the physical and moral saturation with bitterness, and his battered organism and darkened imagination continued to suffer silently beneath the veil of inertia.

It was around midnight when, shaking off the stupor, he opened his eyes once more. He glanced all around. The room was dark and silent. At first he thought himself alone, but he made out the shadows of some loyal friends who had fallen asleep in their chairs.

He did not understand what was happening, but he heard a monotonous, rhythmic murmur of voices—the chorus of prayers issuing from the adjoining room—and through the half-opened door saw a reddish light that sketched a luminous ray upon the floor. And on hearing that terribly sad chorus, and on seeing that light like the glow of a fire, he realized what had happened, and letting loose a cry of grief, tried to get up and go to Aurora's side. But his concerned friends stopped him, so as to prevent a return of the crisis.

"Leave me alone!" Miguel said as he tried to force his way through them. "Let me see her one last time. Am I not a man? I'm strong enough to endure anything, and if I die of grief, it would be better."

But all was in vain: strong arms restrained him and kept him pinned to the bed. He spent the rest of the night in this way, despite the anxieties that consumed him and the sobbing that smothered him.

V.

When he lay down once more, his surprised eyes caught the sight of Aurora, though blurred with his own tears. Upon the wall of the dead woman's chamber hung an enormous mirror that clearly and faithfully reflected her figure. And the widower could see it through the open door.

His beloved lay stretched out on her bed, her face turned to heaven, motionless, with the Olympian stillness of the tomb and with her eyes half-open, as if gazing at this life from the vantage point of the other. Her features were soft and loving; she seemed to console those around her, making them understand that she should not be mourned but rather envied, for happiness now belonged to her. They had dressed her in her bridal gown, as if to say that her soul itself had wed in celestial glory. Her lifeless hands held a crucifix, as if clutching a victory palm. Her bridled wreath was woven into her blonde locks, and the white blossoms of orange flowers that peeped out among the ribbons resembled a starry diadem upon her celestial brow.

The flames of the candles gave out sparks as they rose and fell, and the play of light and shadow on the cadaver's face wrought a strange transformation. At times it seemed that Aurora was breathing, or that she moved her eyelids ever so slightly, or that she sweetly pursed her lips. But the stiffness of her limbs and the stonelike immobility of her breast shattered the optical illusion born of desire. The silence of the night, the candlelight, the endless murmur of prayers, and the half-real, half-fantasy scene that the mirror portrayed seemed purposefully made to inflict indelible wounds upon his imagination.

At dawn the coffin was borne away, and Miguel, wishing to drink the chalice of grief to the dregs, did not hesitate to cry upon seeing it. Pious women took Aurora's remains in their arms and laid her to rest in the casket. A hammer was necessary to fit the lid upon it. Miguel listened to what sounded like tempestuous thunder in the echoes of the hammer blows. It seemed that mass of iron was striking his own temples. He beheld a spinning, luminous disk, then collapsed, senseless.

VI.

When he returned to his senses, it was all over. The house was more silent and mournful than ever. Gone were Aurora's remains, the last vestige of happiness past.

It was in vain that friends and relatives tried to console him, for he did not want to be consoled, tied as he was to his grief with a suicidal fury. He did not speak; he remained sullen and grave. One would have thought that someone had injured him; he seemed to bear a grudge against fate. He no longer cried. His weakened heart beat with a jagged rhythm, like some broken pendulum.

It was only beside his son's cradle that Miguel once more unleashed his torrent of tears. There he cried for the poor creature, so small, weak, and abandoned. The smiling countenance of that tiny angel melted his heart more than his crying would have done. The poor child! He laughed contentedly as if he had not lost a great treasure, as if he had not lost his mother, as if he were not an orphan. A lump formed in Miguel's throat when he pronounced the world *orphan*, and he began to cry unconsolably. How sad a life awaited that child from his earliest days! There would be no exquisite tenderness for him, no minute acts of care such as the other children enjoyed, even the lowest of them, even the poorest. His tiny cradle would never rock to the cooing of soft melodies, fresh and tender. Miguel understood the need to love and care for that innocent child now more than ever, to compensate as much as possible for misfortune's blows. He had to provide a mother's loving solicitude, because the child had none. Miguel had to be his father and mother at the same time.

He always fell into these reflections in his son's presence, there reviving his sorrows to such an extent that he cried and sobbed furiously. The child, frightened to hear his laments, also began to cry, and the young widower saw himself obliged to go away from the crib so as not to agitate the poor creature.

VII.

Since the day that Aurora's body was taken away to the cemetery Miguel went to live in his wife's room, occupying the same bed and resting his head on the same pillows. That reduced space where he had been happy a short time before, those objects that had belonged to Aurora, all of that small world impregnated with her memory, was for Miguel a recollection simultaneously anguishing and delicious. If someone had offered him a kingdom in exchange for them, he would have rejected the suggestion indignantly.

The mirror was one of the most esteemed and valued of those objects. He stayed before it for whole hours each day, staring stubbornly, as if hoping that it would once more reproduce the scene of that tragic sight. But since he revealed his thoughts to no one, it was impossible to fathom the cause of his strange insistence.

"I wish I could see my dear Aurora again," he thought to himself, "even if only once, even if it was the way I saw her that terrible night when she was laid out on her deathbed. Her ghost would not frighten me, because my love exceeds any other sentiment, and neither astonishment nor terror could suffocate my heart's joy in seeing her again!"

And indeed he longed for a vision of Aurora and deliberately exalted his imagination in hopes that it might conjure up one more time the shade of his unforgettable wife. But day after day he waited for a miracle that never came. He angrily decided that the stories of apparitions, stories that circulated among the vulgar, were nothing more than inventions born of fear and superstition.

Meanwhile, time continued to pass with unrelenting speed. Days, weeks, and months went by. The despair of those first moments, the stabbing pain that accompanied the catastrophe, grew duller little by little. It would have been impossible to go on living amid those torments; with time, nature softens the soul's worst anguish and the body's worst suffering. Vital forces reveal themselves as powerful agents against any destructive principle.

"Ah, miserable clay, you cannot even suffer forever!"[4]

That unendurable bitterness suffered a tremendous blow: it was the exhaustion of both body and spirit, the result of so violent a shock. In that situation, Miguel perceived everything through such a dark veil that the world around him seemed to consist of shadows, and everything to be only smoke and mist. It wasn't worth the trouble to raise his head to think, or open his eyes to see, nor lift his hand to act, in a world so false and unstable. Struggle and repose, effort and inertia, all boiled down to a vain illusion, for in a single moment the winds of death sweep the world of human effort, great or small, just as the gusts of the hurricane wipe away clouds from the horizon, whether black as the tempest or golden as the rays of the sun.

Plunged into that despair, he would have preferred to die if it were not for his son. However heartbreaking his thoughts about life, he understood that dejection was a burden that he had to endure, in deference to and for the protection of that innocent creature. He accepted life as an obligation, as a sacrifice. And so love leads those who love to tell themselves: "*I love you so much that for your sake I'm capable of facing death.*" Fatherhood had compelled Miguel to say to his son, with his spirit filled with shadows, and between sighs: "*I love you so much that only for your sake I'm able to face life.*"

One might say that the child was the only thing that bound Miguel to the earth, but that obligation sufficed to keep the disconsolate young man going. But Miguel's self-sacrifice was well rewarded. The child was so beautiful and so sweet! How much he resembled his mother! He was so charming and happy! When he looked at Miguel, he stretched out his tiny pink hands, smiling like an angel and warbling wordlessly, a sound that said nothing but meant a great deal. The widower took his son in his arms, caressed him, kissed him, bathed him in tears. How happy Aurora would be if she could see this moment! Perhaps she would not recognize him! How he had grown so, and how handsome he had become!

In this way, thanks to the forces of nature, the child's love, and the work of time, Miguel's spirit slowly underwent a new transformation. The despair that had turned into dejection now subsided to a melancholy. The memory of Aurora, ever-present in the solitary widower's heart, no longer inflicted torments of agony. True, it made him suffer but now in a soft, romantic way. One might even say that the sadness that possessed him was sweet, for it weighed upon his chest and filled his eyes with tears and inspired a certain languidness of painful intoxication that did not lack for charm.

He no longer looked at his past as something sad but rather as a dream. His earlier life was for him part of a rose-colored illusion, and Aurora herself a mysterious phantom made of light, a phantom that crossed his mind during some delicious ecstasy. Transforming his sorrow in this poetic manner made it easier to bear. And the charm in such an approach lay in the melancholy that he purposely sought as a way of reviving those memories that caused him to fall into such delicious reveries.

VIII.

A year passed in this fashion. Miguel's existence had once more found its equilibrium. Rechanneled and modified, one might say, his grief thus no longer alarmed anyone; it could be his life companion, however long a life God might grant him.

Such was the situation when something unexpected occurred. The widower's sister came to the city for a few days, and she stayed in Miguel's home in the company of her husband and a sister-in-law named Rosa.

Rosa was eighteen years old and extremely charming. She had a smooth, dark complexion like that of Italian women and large, dark eyes like those of Spaniards. Her chestnut hair was full and lustrous, and regardless of whether she combed it meticulously or else carelessly let it fall to her shoulders, it lent her face an unspeakable charm. It seemed that life and joy blossomed around her. Her freshness and youth overflowed; hers was a privileged nature, born to receive happiness and to radiate it in turn.

Miguel had lived with his company for a few days when he noticed that he was only too happy to be near Rosa, that his eyes enjoyed meeting hers, and that he found her accent sweet, her laughter harmonious, and her whole person filled with attractions. When he became aware of his reaction, the sharp sting of remorse penetrated his chest, and, startled as if discovering that he had committed a crime, he fled to the refuge of his child's side.

But out of love for the Miguel, his sister had decided to fan the very ember that he was trying to extinguish, and there were no few episodes when the feminine arts sorely tested Miguel's fidelity and circumspection.

It was unclear whether Rosa had discerned her sister-in-law's plan, but she did certain things that suggested some concerted action between the two. Miguel's situation grew more difficult by the day. The affection that Rosa inspired in him kept growing. At each moment he discovered new charms in his guest, and he felt himself more susceptible to those charms, but he kept up his stern, silent appearance, and no words betrayed the fierce struggles of his heart. How many times, weary of the contest, he ran furiously to lock himself in his room or to take shelter in the shadow of the crib! But it was all fruitless: that budding affection was growing more and more irresistible. In vain he summoned the memories of Aurora to aid him; they remained alive in his heart, but in such a sweet and mystical fashion that they did nothing to halt the growth of a new love.

One day his sister said to him: "I notice that you run away from Rosa."

"Oh?" Miguel replied indifferently.

"Yes," his sister went on, "not because you're distracted, but rather on purpose. My husband and Rosa have observed it and are quite offended."

"Perhaps they consider me a man of poor manners."

"In regard to Rosa, I greatly fear that you are. When you so often walk away from her while she's speaking, or turn your back on her, or answer her sharply, the poor thing goes off to cry where nobody can see her. I've caught her several times with tears in her eyes."

"I'm a brute," Miguel answered. "She's fully justified in thinking me a bad man, but sister, you must forgive me. If I avoid her company, it's because she has a singular effect on me, and one so deep, that it seems to me a crime following the death of Aurora. If this young woman were less enchanting, I would be more courteous to her."

"You mustn't confuse yourself. Suppose that you fall in love with Rosa. What harm would there be in that? Isn't she pretty? Isn't she intelligent? Doesn't she have a good character? She would make an excellent wife and would very much love your son."

"Don't speak to me of that matter. I swore to Aurora that I would not love again, nor give my son a stepmother, and I must comply."

His sister laughed at these high-sounding phrases and tried to persuade him that such obstacles hardly mattered. The vow to never love again was void, she said, given that compliance was not a matter of choice. As for the child, there was no reason to suppose that Rosa was the child's executioner; rather, they had every reason to hope that she was a guardian angel, given her education, character, and sentiments.

Her arguments had a certain effect on Miguel's spirit, and from that day on he became more accessible in his treatment of Rosa. And for that reason she unfurled all her charms and delights, happy and relieved to see so visible a change.

In this way a new love imperceptibly took control of Miguel's heart. He no longer rejected it with horror, no longer considered it a crime. He looked for ways of excusing himself in his own eyes. Aurora was dead: in what way was he injuring her? Moreover, he would never forget her, for it was impossible to wipe away that sweet memory from the depths of his soul. As for his son, he would find in Rosa a second mother, for the sentiments of that striking young woman were as beautiful as her appearance.

But despite his reflections, remorse pricked his conscience. He could not enter his bedroom in peace. Everything reminded him of Aurora. That furniture, those drapes: all those objects held something of his wife, and it seemed that some sort of murmur issued from them, an unintelligible voice that blended complaint and threat. When he lay on the bed, he was assailed by attacks of fear that kept him awake. At times it seemed that by reaching a hand into the shadows he would find the cold, lifeless body of his dead companion.

The mirror still caused him intense fear. When his eyes happened to glance at it, he forced them to look elsewhere. At night he slept with his face to the opposite wall so as not to have the mirror before him.

But despite everything, he did not resolve to change rooms. It seemed to Miguel that to abandon his late wife's quarters would have been an act of ingratitude and treachery.

IX.

But when he was with Rosa, he forgot everything. Because she was so pleasant and charming, she made all his anxieties disappear, just as the sun rising in the east dissipates all the terrors that beset those souls terrified by night shadows.

One evening Miguel, on leaving the family *tertulia*,[5] headed mechanically to the garden. He feared the moment when he would reenter his room and he wanted to postpone that entrance by a few moments.

The moon was shining like a snowball in the sky, against the silvery dots of the stars. The plants reposed in silent slumber, unruffled by even the slightest of breezes. The flowers' corollas looked pale under the rays of the night sky. Everything around him lay wrapped in peace and mystery.

The fountain that stood out amid the foliage made a rhythmic murmur that invited dreams. Miguel sat beside it and, placing his head in his hands, fell into deep meditation. He thought about Aurora, about his son, about Rosa, and those thoughts were at times sad, at other moments joyful. He remained there, lost in his own mind for a considerable time, until something woke him from his revery, a sound that he perceived in the garden grove. He looked carefully and discovered the silhouette of a woman. Was it his sister or Rosa? Oh, if only it were Rosa!

And indeed it was Rosa. What brought her to the garden at this hour? Had she come by chance or on purpose? Perhaps she came as he did, to give herself to her dreams, impelled by some force superior to her own will. As his heart beat with emotion, he said: "Rosa!"

She stifled a cry of surprise and made to leave.

"What?" Miguel continued with a sweet voice. "Are you leaving? Does my presence bother you?"

"No," said Rosa with trembling voice, "but it's late, and I should not be here."

"Now that we've met each other by accident, would it anger you to grant me a few moments?"

"Only if they are brief. . . ."

"Well, then," Miguel said hurriedly, and taking her hand, which she gave him without hesitation, "I must tell you many things, so many that I don't know how to express them all. Without doubt they can be condensed to very few, only a few: I love you with all my heart, with my entire life."

Rosa did not respond.

"You remain silent," Miguel went on. "Am I to believe that your silence means indifference? I know that I am not worthy of you. Perhaps I am a brute who has gone mad dreaming of a happiness that God never granted him."

That same silence followed these words, but Rosa's lips trembled as though struggling to say something that she could not pronounce.

"Rosa," Miguel insisted, "it's imperative that you tell me if in the recesses of your heart you harbor some sentiment corresponding to my own; for I ought to know, I have a right to find out, and it's urgent that I learn the truth. Do you love me? Do I inspire in you nothing but disdain? In the name of heaven, speak to me."

"Ah," said Rosa, making a supreme effort, and with a broken voice that was almost imperceptible, "you ask me if I love you? I loved you before you loved me, from the moment I met you."

And so saying, she withdrew her hand from Miguel's and ran away toward her quarters.

X.

At the end of the day that the civil contract was celebrated,[6] Miguel headed to his room at midnight. Despite his happiness, once he found himself alone, he was overcome with a profound terror, one that he found impossible to shake off. His infidelity was consummated; he had broken his vow.

By a strange coincidence the memory of those moments came back to him, all those details concerning Aurora's death. Who at the time would have told him that he would be so traitorous, so thankless!

He opened the door to his room and cast a fearful glance all around. It had once been Aurora's room; there she had lived; there she had died; there, in her final moments, she had received his vow never to love another woman again. And what had happened? He had fallen in love once more and had taken a second wife. He was confused and thought he deserved to be punished. This was how he returned a love so tender, so enormous, so noble, that very love that Aurora had professed to him! She was watching him from eternity. What a shame! Where was he to hide his face?

Turning these matters over in his mind, he went to bed deeply worried and turned out the light. He turned his face to the wall as always and tried to sleep. Smiles soon took the place of his sad thoughts, and filled with emotion as he remembered Rosa's eyes, and saw them again, fixed to his own with tenderness. And he heard the echo of that voice that said to him: "I loved you before you loved me. I loved you from the moment I met you."

At last he was able to sleep, now with a smile on his lips and joy in his heart.

Several hours of tranquil sleep had passed when suddenly he awoke, as if roused by some invisible hand. He opened his eyes and to his surprise found the room brightly illuminated. Intuitively, Miguel turned his head in search of that light's place of origin.

His terrified eyes settled on the mirror that he had so dreaded. It was illuminated, and from it came that clear light that filled the room. Four enormous candles cast out a reddish glow that was reflected in the mirror.[7] In the space between them he saw a bed adorned with a white spread that hung down over the sides. On top of the bed lay Aurora, stretched out in her bridal gown and with a crown of orange blossoms on her head. Her ashen and immobile face seemed contracted in an expression of extreme pain. Teardrops glistened on the long eyelashes that fell over her faded cheeks.

The widower felt the blood freeze in his veins, his hair stood on end, and his teeth chattered volubly. He sat up in bed at the sight of this eerie scene. In vain Miguel tried to turn away his eyes, but a supernatural power called to them, drawing them back. In vain he tried to scream, but his voice drowned in his convulsed throat.

The vision gradually faded away, and everything lay submerged in darkness once more. But little by little the mirror began to glow again, and the same objects reappeared. In that terrifying frame Miguel beheld a new and different sight, one that bore the stamp of reality.

It was his son's room. The child was sleeping peacefully in his crib. One of his arms rested on his head; his locks of hair curled over his cheeks, and as he dreamed he smiled, as if beholding some beautiful vision.

Suddenly a white form appeared next to the crib. It resembled a thin vapor, but slowly its features took shape. It was a woman dressed in white. Who was she? He stared at her in astonishment. It was Aurora, as pale and somber as she had been on her deathbed. She leaned over the crib, briefly kissed the child on the forehead, took him up in her arms, then disappeared with her precious bundle.

At that moment the light vanished, and the room was drenched in darkness.

XI.

Miguel remained terrified for a moment amid the shadows, with his face turned and his eyes fastened on the mirror. In the night's silence his breathing sounded slow and labored, like a smothered cry of anguish, and his teeth gave off a chattering sound as his jaw trembled. The bed itself, brought to life by the spasms of his body, produced a sinister clacking.

When he recovered somewhat, he ran his hand across his forehead. Had he been the victim of a nightmare? The terrifying scenes that he had beheld: had they been the hallucinatory fruit of some dream? No, he was certain he had been awake. Had he gone mad? Perhaps. Whatever the case, what was happening to him was truly horrible.

He lit the candle. A fixed idea tormented him: his son! Miguel leapt from the bed, grabbed the light, opened the door, and rushed from the room. He crossed the dark and empty hallway without noticing the cold draft that lashed his face and made the candlelight flicker.

With a face as pale and stricken as if he had committed a crime, he reached his son's room and tiptoed toward the crib. Bursting with emotion he lifted the curtains and bent down to kiss the adored child.

But finding him stiff and cold, Miguel let loose a heart-rending scream and fell to the floor as if struck by lightning.

The child was dead!

Nieves

I.

It is a fact that the town of Tequila is famous as a center for the alcohol that bears its name. It is also a fact that something else commends it to the tourist: it once served as the nation's fortress and bulwark against the invasion of the Nayarit savages.[1] People prayed the "Hail, Mary" in that terrible year of 1873;[2] even today I thrill to hear its sound, so much like the voice of a friend. But now swallows had taken refuge in the tops of the orange trees, high above the adobe walls; they chirped with joy to see me, just like in old times.

And so I came to my old family home there on the main plaza. An aunt of mine was living there, my mother's sister. I dismounted at the entrance and walked inside, leading my horse by the bridle. Only the servants came out to receive me; my aunt, along with her two sons, had gone to visit her ranchos. While waiting for them to return, I strolled around the sorrow-filled house. Except for a fat orange tree in the middle of the patio, now joyous with the sound of nesting birds, everything looked altogether changed. Time had passed for this tequila center the way it passes for the body of a beautiful woman, sowing decay and destruction everywhere. Everything looked old and exhausted, as if vandal hordes had come this way: the vandal hordes of the years, alas, more blind and cruel than the followers of Alaric and Genseric.[3]

The house's furnishings and overall layout, so different from those of earlier days, put the finishing touches on its disfiguration. In the living room, gone was the furniture of ivory-encrusted cedar frame and white-linen upholstery that I had once known. In their place stood more modern versions lacking in both character and tradition. The room where my grandfather slept had been converted into an office; the quarters of my mother, my sister, and me were now a pharmacy with doors that opened to the street. The heavy and enormous wooden table had disappeared from the dining room. I had sat at that table, as had the sons, sons-in-law, and grandchildren of the house's original owner. In the corral, the scene of my first equestrian attempts, there was only a pair of weak and motionless horses, standing like statues alongside the crib . . . hardly the spirited animals whose powerful hooves had once reverberated against the stone pavement.

After having a look around, I headed for the broad corral that led to the patio, and, taking a seat in a leather chair, I continued with my reflections. Scenes passed through my mind with such clarity and precision of detail that they seemed like events of the present. It was daybreak, and I could see my grandfather waking up his sons and me. We rose to the light of tallow lamps and went to the cattle stables. It was Sunday, and the house was full of servants who had come to receive their wages. My grandfather sat at the head of an enormous oak table, while to his right a secretary read off the payroll list, as another assistant loudly called out the name of each worker, the balance of his account, and his due payment in money, meat, and corn. For this process, bags full of money covered the table, with still more coins in gourds and frying pans for the benefit of the rustics, who stared at those treasures with respect and astonishment. Still other assistants distributed the corn by means of wooden measuring cups that were first heaped full, then scraped level. A slaughtered ox had been cut into quarters, then hung on metal hooks in a portable cabinet. Sliced by a pot-bellied butcher's sharp knife, it provided the workers with the coveted ration of meat that the booming voice of the assistant had just decreed.

The sudden sound of horses at the house's entrance roused me from these meditations—almost. I could still see my grandfather returning from the field, followed by his workers. He rode a huge dapple-gray mule, strong and sure-footed. Grandfather had on a white jacket and dark, flannel pants. On his head he wore a white scarf, clean and ironed, its tips dangling over the nape of his neck; above that, a lead-gray felt hat of wide brim and imposing rectangular crown. The huge spurs fastened to his high leather riding boots had small steel chains that jingled as the animal moved. When he dismounted, servants hurried to remove the spurs and to relieve him of the whip he carried in his right hand. The tall, robust figure of the septuagenarian towered imperiously over the coterie of servants and exuded both natural kindness and a manly energy.

Then the memory abated. The horses entered the corridor, and I went out to welcome my aunt and cousins as they returned to the rancho. They received me with lavish displays of happiness; we hugged tightly and then went inside the house. Once dinner was over my aunt led me into the room she had prepared as my quarters using the finest available furnishings.

When I woke up the next morning the sun was shining splendidly over the horizon. I walked over to the window and took in the view, that same gorgeous panorama that had so captivated me in my younger days. The enormous hill of El Tequila stood before me, its dark green mass rising high above the roofs of the recently painted house that lined the other side of the plaza. It stood out at many leagues' distance, particularly the conical peak that sat upon it like a crown, and which is known by the name of Tetilla.[4] Thick forests cover the mountain's broad foothills, while sparse vegetation grows along the higher regions, and when winter comes snow adorns its peaks like some sign of the age of this huge volcanic body.

My cousin got up early to supervise work in the fields, and I ate breakfast alone with my aunt. As I sat here I kept recalling past scenes, memories no longer those of a single voice but rather as a rich chorus. At this side of the table sat my grandfather, here my father, over there my mother, here my sister, and here too I myself. In my grandfather's time a huge clay pot stood at the center of the table. It was covered with a tray and, on top of that, a dipper with a cup handle used to draw out the frothy milk it contained. My grandfather himself served breakfast, and as soon as it was over we all stood, and imitating his example and his lead, we prayed in thanksgiving to Providence, just as we did at the end of every meal.

I was still eating when Don Santos, a wealthy old friend of the family, came to greet me with his impeccable courtesy and to invite me to visit his properties. Not having anything else to do, I was happy to accept his proposition, and taking advantage of a carriage waiting for us, we were soon underway.

II.

The rancho of Don Santos is called La Florida, and it lies two leagues from Tequila. My host notified me when we reached the boundaries of his property. At that precise moment we began to see extensive and well-tended fields of agave plants[5] on both sides of the road, fields that showed the hand of a skilled cultivator.

"How many plants do you have?" I asked.

"Around a million," he replied.

"Amazing . . ."

"Not so much," Don Santos responded. "Your own grandfather came to own more than three million."

The truth is that forty years ago my grandfather was the most renowned producer of alcohol in the entire state. His fortune became immense, but during the Reform War the exactions of one revolutionary band or another had reduced that fortune considerably.[6]

"You're quite wealthy," I continued.

"Not yet," he objected, somewhat pretentiously, "but I'm hoping to become so. The life of the mezcal planter is difficult while waiting for the plants to begin producing. They are slow to reach maturity."

"How long do you have to wait?"

"Between ten and twelve years. Any money invested in them remains completely useless during that time. Their plantings cover the fields. Planting from seed is expensive. And during their period of growth, the ground has to be plowed and cleared every year. All this requires large amounts of capital."

"But when it's all over," I remarked, "when it's time to distill the alcohol, the operation pays handsomely."

"It's true. That is when the mezcal planter reaps the reward for his hard work and sacrifice. Only the business of mining yields better returns, although you must weigh those against the disadvantage of hazardous labor, something not found in our enterprise."

The carriage rolled slowly and unsteadily over the rocky ground. Don Santos halted our progress every so often to point out his vast domain and to provide me with technical explanations. As we rose along the hill slopes, we saw land covered with mezcal plants in straight, parallel, and symmetrical rows, their large, tough leaves a bluish green. They covered these hills like a monstrous net that extended all the way to the horizon.

My companion explained which land was best for planting. He showed me the mezcal seeds, born at the base of the older plants.[7] He pointed out plants of all different ages and conditions, including both those whose time was ripe and those that were still immature, those that received care and those that did not. In this way we eventually reached the core of the hacienda.

We left the carriage and went inside the main house. Don Santos had done marvelous things here. In front of the house, he had created a large plaza surrounded by rock walls. It led to a broad entrance that was closed at night by means of a huge corridor, at one extreme of which stood a chapel and at the other a school. At that moment the chapel's construction was nearly complete. I observed that it followed an unknown form of architecture, one perhaps invented by the stone mason who shaped the heads of the chapel's columns. He had adorned them with flowers, birds, serpents, and a veritable multitude of exquisite details nestled among its leaves; all of this would have been anathema in a true Corinthian column. The proprietor gazed appreciatively at this rich variety of forms and took visible satisfaction in pointing out the work to me.

As the blessing of the chapel was at hand, he invited me to attend the ceremony.

In the school we found three half-naked children. Crude charcoal pencils in hand, they copied down the letters from the poster that hung on the wall. The teacher was a carpenter who busied himself in varnishing a table destined for the office, while his students reviewed their lesson.

Nothing noteworthy distinguished the interior of the house. A living room, some bed chambers, a dining room, a kitchen, a corral, and extensive stables: all were devoid of luxury but wide and well ventilated.

When the visit had ended, Don Santos looked at me with a mischievous eye and said: "I still have to show you the best part of my hacienda."

"What is that?"

"The pretty girls."

"Seriously!"

"We have seven here. The blacksmith's daughter, the daughter of the carpenter, four sisters who live outside the gate, and a fifteen-year-old servant whom everyone calls the Virgin of La Florida."

"So, she's really pretty, you say?"

"You can judge with your own eyes."

"Then let's go and have a look at her."

"No, not yet. We must proceed in order. The girl who lives closest is the blacksmith's daughter."

The smith in question kept his shop close by, and we soon arrived. This resident Vulcan was at that moment busy hammering out a glowing piece of iron that an inexperienced apprentice held over an anvil by means of pincers. Upon seeing us the maestro greeted us courteously, albeit without stopping his labors for fear of letting the iron cool. Don Santos led me into a kitchen on the pretext of offering me some water; but we found no one there. The girl had gone to the stream to fill the pitcher.

With the first stage of our enterprise a failure, we now headed to the home of the carpenter. As we approached, I was struck by the darkness of the place. The carpenter spoke to us from his bed, for it turned out that he was sick with fever. Upon hearing the news Don Santos was struck by the idea of contagion and dragged me away.

It was at that moment that the village *cura* arrived to hear the stricken man's confession.[8] He wore a straw hat and rode a spirited horse that tossed the poor man high in the saddle as it trotted along. The tips of the padre's feet barely reached the stirrups. It was clear that the journey had been hard on him, a fact written onto his countenance. The sun, coupled with exhaustion, had burned his face and caused him to sweat copiously. He halted the steed, dismounted, and gently saluted us. From beneath his cassock he produced a small vial that he had wrapped in a blue pouch. This he hung around his neck and unhesitatingly entered into the carpenter's house.

Don Santos and I looked at each other in astonishment. We had entered that hovel without knowing what we would find, driven merely by the desire to look over the rustic beauty who lived there; but this had not been incentive enough to stop us from fleeing when we learned of the disease.

The saintly priest, to the contrary, had come with the express purpose of hearing the afflicted man's confessionand had dropped everything without a moment's hesitation. Sun-burned, covered with sweat, at full risk of contagion, this determined priest entered the house, eager to save the man's soul. What miracles religion produces! What great deeds come from virtue!

As I thought about the matter, I mechanically followed Don Santos as he crossed the plaza and exited the gate, eventually reaching a miserable hut. We entered with a "*buenos días*" and were answered by a chorus of different voices. It was here that the four beautiful girls lived.

One of them was patting out tortillas. She ground the corn on a stone metate, flattened and stretched the dough between her hands, then placed the tortillas on a clay *comal* resting on stones, beneath which burned the powerful flames of a wood fire.[9] This particular girl did not cut an appealing figure.

Another of the sisters busied herself with straining coagulated milk in a basket to make cheese. There was nothing seductive in her face, either.

A third sister was seated on the floor with her legs drawn up and wrapped in her *rebozo*.[10] Though hardly beautiful, her face was pleasant enough, but the poor girl was suffering from intermittent fever and had a yellowish complexion.[11]

Huddled in the corner of the room, her back to the light, was the fourth sister. Don Santos had her turn her face toward us. The poor girl suffered from inflamed eyes and cried incessantly. Unquestionably, she was in no condition to entice. Of the four sisters whose beauty my host had extolled, not one had been worth the trouble.

Our visit had been brief. We enjoyed a bit of cheese tacos with these young ladies. We conversed a while, and we advised them to take certain medications for their illnesses: an infusion of *hoja de gigante* for the fever and sap from the heart of the mesquite tree dissolved in water for the eye malady.[12] On that note we took our leave.

"So far we're out of luck," Don Santos said to me as we were leaving. "After all, you haven't seen one beautiful face among the girls I've shown you. The best looking are either sick or out somewhere. You must think me a man of poor taste. But wait until the Virgin of La Florida redeems my reputation."

"We'll see," I replied.

The truth was that after searching for so long I was beginning to think that Don Santos was indeed a man of dubious taste. I had little faith that the Virgin of La Florida, as he called her, was superior to the beauties we had just seen.

We passed by two or three huts before eventually stopping.

"Good morning, Doña Petra," said Don Santos.

"Good morning, *señor amo*,"[13] answered a woman standing at the door of that miserable shack. She was an old woman with red hair, ugly and with her head wrapped in filthy rags.

"Where is Cruz?" my companion asked.

I thought that he was referring to a woman, but to my surprise I saw that he was talking about a man, for upon hearing his voice an old fellow emerged from the hut: tall, brawny, one-eyed, and smoking a long cigar made of corn husks.[14]

"At your orders, *señor amo*," answered the old man.

"Here before you," said Don Santos, "you have the famous Cruz Analco."

"At Your Mercy's orders,"[15] the old man repeated.

"Well," said Don Santos as we entered the hut, with me trailing behind. "Where is the Virgin? This *frastero* wants to meet her."[16]

"She's out feeding the chickens," said Petra. "I'll go call her."

While Petra went out to fetch the Virgin, the three of us entered the hut.

"In a few words," Don Santos told me, "I'm going to fill you in on this family. Petra is the blood aunt of the Virgin and is married. Her friend Analco lives *en mala amistad*, her husband notwithstanding.[17] They all live together."

"God Almighty!" I exclaimed. "And the husband lives with them?"

"At your command," said a man who at that moment appeared at the door of the hut.

"No one called you, Jesús," said Don Santos.

"But I heard this gentleman asking for me," the newcomer objected, pointing his finger at me.

"No one needs you here, friend!" Analco shouted. "Stay outside!"

Jesús immediately disappeared. He was scrawny, dark-skinned, and shabbily dressed, to judge from appearances more humiliated than can be imagined, the very image of the "poor devil."

"He's the husband of Petra," Analco said with disdain.

"I continue with my account," Don Santos dryly interrupted. "Petra is the sister of the Virgin's mother. But the Virgin is now an orphan, and Petra has assumed responsibility for her by taking her into the family. The Virgin has no living relation other than her sister, but since that unworthy sister was thrown into the street, it was hardly appropriate that Nieves continue living with her."

"Yes," Analco added, "the girl took refuge with us to avoid coming to ruin."

"A fine refuge, by my faith!" I replied.

At that moment Petra returned. From the bottom of a basket she took a printed calico petticoat and a pair of blue taffeta shoes.

"I'm going to take these clothes to that conceited girl," said the aunt as she went out once more.

For a good while we sat silently, for Don Santos had concluded his account, and I myself had nothing to say. The silence was only interrupted when Aunt Petra returned to announce: "Come in, niña. Has there ever been such an insolent girl? Come in, your amo wants to say hello, and to have you meet another gentleman."

The girl entered little by little, held back by a profound timidity. She had put on the brightly colored petticoat and blue shoes. A rebozo almost entirely covered her face. Don Santos rose from his chair, and approaching her with familiarity, removed the rebozo, saying:

"Say hello, don't be a *ranchera*.[18] The gentleman wants to meet you."

"May the Lord grant Your Mercy a good day," said the blushing girl as she extended a hand.

"Good day," I returned, looking her directly in the face.

White-skinned, blonde, blue-eyed, she breathed modesty and shyness with her entire being. Her oval face was perfect; enchanting dimples adorned her cheeks. Her small carnation of a mouth revealed white teeth. Her nose was well shaped. Her forehead, somewhat small, harmonized gracefully with her other features. Her thick eyebrows ran together to create a severe expression that contrasted with her sweet eyes. She was tall and slender, evidently at that age when a girl begins to grow. Her voice too was sweet, even vibrant. Don Santos had not deceived me: the Virgin of La Florida was very beautiful indeed.

"What is your name, niña?" I asked her. "And how old are you?"

"I'm called María de las Nieves, señor, and I am your servant. I'm about to turn fifteen."

"A pretty name and a pretty age," Don Santos observed. "Isn't that so?"

"Most certainly," I replied. "It all fits with the beauty of this child."

"Does she strike you as pretty?" Don Santos asked me.

"Yes, very much so," I replied.

Nieves covered her face with her hands, but finding no way to avoid our gaze she turned away from us.

"Ill-mannered child," said Analco. "Don't turn your back to these gentlemen."

Aunt Petra added, "Take your hands off your face!"

And since Nieves neither turned around nor showed her face, her aunt forcibly spun her on her feet to face us and pulled down her hands.

"Let her be," I said. "She's right to be bashful."

"Come here, *niña*," Don Santos exclaimed. "Sit beside me."

He pointed to a place next to him on the bed of *tapextle* that doubled as a chair.[19]

Nieves resisted, but her aunt pulled her down by the petticoat.

"Are you afraid of me?" Don Santos asked.

Nieves did not reply. Don Santos then took her rich, golden locks in his hand and exclaimed as he showed them to me: "Pretty hair, isn't it?"

The poor girl remained as flushed as a poppy flower and refused to raise her eyes from the floor. She stayed immobile as a statue. And she remained that way for a long time. Analco, Petra, and Don Santos kept the conversation going with talk about trivialities. I chimed in from time to time. Nieves neither opened her lips nor dared to look at us.

As all of this was happening, it hurt me to see that beautiful girl mired in such a poisonous environment. Everything about her harmonized: her delicate features, her slender waist, her well-shaped hands, her silvery smile, her eyes like those of a gazelle.[20] Nothing about her clashed; her entire being moved in a single rhythm. I could not explain to myself how such a creature could have been born to that repulsive family. But after all, don't lilies bloom in mud puddles? There was no resemblance whatsoever between Nieves and her aunt Petra; they formed polar opposites of the human race, beauty versus ugliness. Who could explain it? And what dark future awaited that creature? An orphan, sister to a fallen woman, living beside an aunt who provided the worst of examples, beside an utterly immoral man like Analco, and beside another utterly contemptible man, Jesús: she had nowhere to cast her eyes for protection or turn her ears for sound advice. At the same time, Don Santos was an old lecher, one of those individuals who violate and trample upon young women to satisfy their appetites. Every time he looked at the poor girl I saw the flame of satanic desire in the hacendado's eyes.

There is an unfortunate fact about Mexico, a land of free institutions, a land that has proclaimed even the humblest people to be free from the tyranny of the powerful. Even now there exists a sizable number of rural proprietors who actively retain the honor and ancient privileges of the haciendas; namely, to treat their servants as possessions, as if they were the bonded slaves of long ago. They administer justice with their own hands, subject their people to tortures like the stocks, reduce their wages, pay them with corn, with scrip, with mere paper. They force their servants to consume what the hacienda sells and at prices that the hacendado determines. And as the height of injustice, they despoil their servants' wives and daughters, a misfortune that strikes at the bosom of the family and at the innermost heart of the *campesino*.[21]

Don Santos was one of those cruel and arbitrary hacendados who abuse their position to terrorize the people who inhabit their estates. And as for those proud and honorable souls who refuse to bear this yoke: well, they are branded as thieves and then ignominiously banished from the property.

At the same time, it occurred to me that Petra and Analco were sufficiently vile to aid Don Santos in his wicked designs. There was too much in their language and behavior toward their amo, too much of baseness and servility to think them innocent. Moreover, their licentious lives lent even further weight to this suspicion.

Why is it that some people are born destined for misfortune? Why was Nieves an orphan, and why had she been exposed to corruption and perfidy, instead of finding herself in a virtuous and protective home? The deeper I became absorbed in these thoughts, the more I took an interest in that poor girl's welfare. But Don Santos misinterpreted my glances.

"Well, now," he mused, "it seems that Nieves has really caught your attention. You can't stop looking at her. You're going to make me jealous. What do you say about this, Nieves?" And so saying, he laughed out loud.

"In reality," I answered in all seriousness as I broke out of my reverie, "I find her altogether fascinating."

On hearing me she lifted her blue eyes from the ground and looked at me timidly for a moment. My heart stood still. How to control the effect that her beauty and innocence had upon me? I was too sentimental in those days, I confess, and I further confess that I was a slave to that sweetest of magic, that enchanting, almost irresistible influence that God gave to beautiful women.

We took our leave. Saying goodbye to Nieves, Don Santos grasped her hand and held it for a long time, even though the girl tried to free herself from his grip. Aunt Petra and Analco scolded her, telling her that the amo didn't have malaria.

III.

On the road back to Tequila, Don Santos and I talked for a long time about Nieves.

"You were right to call her the Virgin of La Florida," I told him. "She's a very beautiful girl."

"Then by chance do you concede that I have good taste?"

I gave him his due credit.

"It was only a short while ago that this family came to my hacienda. And I'm certain you can understand why I'm happy about it."

"That's how I see it."

"That rogue Analco and the old woman are sharp enough to see that I'm interested in her, and I can swear that they're making the most of it. They ask me for assistance at every moment. Living quarters, land for planting, money: I give them whatever they ask for. Only a few days ago the authorities over in Tequila threw Analco in prison for theft. I managed to have him set free and put up bail for good conduct."

"And yet you believe him to be an honest man?"

"What am I supposed to believe? I'm convinced that he's a cunning rascal. I think he's capable of anything: robbery, murder, arson, whatever crime you care to mention."

"It's not hard to imagine him implicating you."

"I've already thought about it. But in such instance the worst that could happen would be that I would have to give him some money. Conversely, I can dispose of Analco as I would a slave."

Building upon that point, Don Santos went on to explain, and with the most profound cynicism, his perverse intentions regarding Nieves. I said: "Don't her youth, her beauty, and her vulnerability inspire pity in you?"

"My friend," he replied, "she is one of those poor creatures whom destiny has condemned to a bad end. However you look at it, Nieves is fated to misfortune. She was born to that fate. And as such, it's not I who tosses her into the abyss, but rather her own bad luck."

It was in vain that I tried to convince Don Santos that it would be cowardice on his part to take advantage of these same circumstances, that he should dedicate himself to some other adventure, in which he could at least take pride in victory after the battle; and that it would be far more satisfying to turn the poor girl into a happy soul by combating her evil star, than to drag her into disgrace. All was in vain. Don Santos laughed in my face, telling me that I was spouting nonsense and then concluded by insinuating that I spoke out of envy and that I would do the same if I were in his position. I insisted no further, and we changed the subject. Presently we fell into a prolonged silence.

Don Santos was an old man, well beyond fifty, heavy-set, with thick brow, and with vulgar features. He wore his hair uncut and unkempt. His beard too was wild, full, and uncombed; nestled within it were white hairs, like the quills of a porcupine. His hands, yellowed by cigar smoke, displayed long black fingernails. So too his way of dressing was off-putting and repugnant. Perhaps more than anything he seemed pitiless and corrupt. To my eyes he resembled a hawk circling in on a timid white dove.

It was the hottest part of the day, and, traveling under a burning sun and nearly suffocated by the heat of the air, we at last made it back to town. I was relieved to say goodbye to Don Santos, for I was tired of his company.

IV.

It is, generally speaking, the custom of the towns in this region to offer the outsider all sorts of invitations and excursions to the countryside. Generous and amiable neighbors compete with one another to entertain and court him. These acts of benevolence are almost a matter of self-esteem on the part of the humble residents, whether it be the offer of providing accommodations or an invitation to a dance or dinner. This generous disposition toward hospitality constitutes one of the defining (and certainly one of the most agreeable) features of our small settlements. They call to mind those patriarchal customs that existed under the Spanish Empire, whereby the guest was considered sacred, almost to the point of becoming the object of a cult. And they contrast pleasantly with the greed and selfishness that are slowly taking control of the capital.[22] However, all situations have their good and bad sides. It is civilization's illness to produce, among other vices, a coldness of affect, one that reduces brotherly love among residents of the same place. But small towns, despite their open-handed hospitality, have their souls seared by a hundred painful sores that make life difficult and sorrowful. In this way, for example, slander and jealousy fill the hearts and mouths of the villages, where people watch, ridicule, and condemn everything in the most inhuman manner, turning everyone's existence into a chorus of hatred and discord.

Any traveler who has spent much time in a village is bound to confirm these observations, but said faults are less evident to the person who, like a bird of passage, only stops long enough to shake off the dust of the road and catch his breath before resuming the journey. So it was that I, who had gone alone to Tequila with the idea of rekindling warm memories and with no intention of remaining for long, had no time for anything beyond visiting familiar places and for refilling my heart with that romantic pleasure that comes from contemplating a fortunate past. Owing to such favorable circumstances, I had the good fortune of seeing only the more attractive part of the picture, and not the painful impressions that its defects could bring.

During my visit I was cosseted and fussed over by relatives and by friends of the house, and in a manner so determined and so courteous that I will never be able to forget. I went to one rancho after another; I hiked through the foothills of Tequila and climbed down to the bottom of La Barranca, through which run the dark, roaring waters of the Río de Santiago.[23] More than anything, I was delighted not so much by what was new but rather by those panoramas that I had seen before. I contemplated them not with my physical eyes, but with that spiritual melancholy that knows how to find such magic and such colorings in the objects at hand.

One of my cousins, who was aware of my inclinations, suggested that we visit the renowned hacienda El Potrero, which lies three leagues from Tequila, at about two-thirds the full depth of La Barranca. I was overjoyed to receive the invitation, and at daybreak the following morning we set out on horseback, accompanied by our servants.

The trail began at ground level, but little by little we came upon small mounds of rock, each one more rugged than the previous, and eventually leading to the edge of an immense basin that stretched out for entire leagues in dark fields and winding paths. It is impossible to make out the nature of this abyss when seen from above. From its upper edge it appears as a cavity formed by sterile and descending slopes; the eyes perceive nothing other than sharp-peaked boulders, rocky depths, and at intervals a series of yellowish and infertile table lands. From time to time on the slopes, we could vaguely make out what appeared to be greenish traces of that fungus that grows on the damp walls of wells, or scraggly circles of lichen that form on the stones' surfaces. But this desolate panorama is a mere optical illusion. Seen close up, those greenish stains in fact prove to be oases of exuberant vegetation that sway with the zephyrs of paradise. Similarly, the gullies that at a distance appear as no more than dark wrinkles conceal an efflorescence of plants in which nature, frenetic and delirious, brings forth all manner of growth. The openings that from far away seem little more than drab, dark cavities on the sloping hillside, and that descend without rhyme or reason into points unknown, are in reality dizzying precipices covered with fronds, bowers, fruit, and flowers, all of which become even more abundant the farther one descends into the depths of the earth.

That descent begins with a gentle incline. Very soon the trail becomes almost as vertical as a ladder. We headed downward along narrow passageways through which the horses had to proceed in single file. The path breaks into angular zigzags, like the image a lightning bolt traces in the heavens and becomes rocky and harsh like the bed over which a torrent of water has passed. We advanced step by step, holding tight the bridle to keep the animals from tripping or sliding. To the left and to the right, before and behind, we stared at how the green moss completely fills all available space, scarcely allowing a bit of blue sky to peep through here and there amid the dense foliage. A thousand stirring sounds reached my ears in confusion, all formed by the breath of the wind that hums as it collides with the rugged patches of La Barranca, whether by the swaying of the branches, by the rustling of the banana plants, or by the babbling water of the streams. Those streams are limpid, and their murmurs break out everywhere as they tumble into the abyss, turning to foam as they crash upon the rocks. In so doing the water becomes a shower of pearls and emerges from the channels of granite to form splendid cataracts. Birds peep amid the branches, and in those places where the woods are greenest and densest, one hears the delightful songs of these winged musicians who unintentionally intone their hymns of liberty and of rejoicing over nature.

As we descended the heat intensified, the air became thin, and the vegetation grew more abundant.[24] Mosquitoes fly silently and place themselves in abundance between the eye and its object, the way that certain illnesses cause a stain upon the retina. And from time to time, with no more sound than a tiny buzz, they fasten themselves to the skin and bite furiously, in so doing inflicting a sting that nothing other than fire or alcohol can calm. We saw lizards running across the path, hiding themselves in the cracks of the boulders. Frightened squirrels fled before us, their bushy, felt-like tails raised high, while a few snakes slithered rapidly across the ground like animated lines of green and glimmered as they lost themselves in the brush that lined the path. The panorama changed unexpectedly at each moment. Now it opened or closed in the rocky basin; now it rose at the top of a hill, towering above the deep green valleys that appear at the traveler's feet. Glancing at times through the branches and the climbing plants that cling to the path's edge, we discovered tremendous abysses in whose depths we dimly perceived running streams. Banana groves filled the folds and wrinkles of the basin. The sage impregnated the air with its penetrating scent. The plum trees raised their squalid bare branches in the air; they resembled the arms of a beggar in India. Ivy, with its blue and red flowers, covered the yellow trunks of the trees like enamel, alleviating the monotony of the rocks or the fallen leaves of the underbrush.

Beside the road we came upon the famous site called El Chorro, where water gushes from an enormous boulder. The edges of La Barranca are giant ledges sharpened to a point. From the rock, arid and bare, issues a thick spring of the purest bubbling water, which falls from an enormous height into a basin that by its own force it has carved out of the hard surface, constantly boiling over as the water strikes against it. The sound that this waterfall produces, repeated and amplified through echoes, deafens by its sheer volume and prevents any communication between those who witness it, unless one of the parties places his mouth against the other's ear and shouts his words directly. The water is warm and inviting to the touch. It roils in the limited space of its cauldron, then runs down the sides of La Barranca and tumbles into its depths. The vegetation that springs therefrom is so profuse that it obscures the light of day, producing a cascade in mysterious shadows, something that notably heightens the scenic beauty and majesty. Whole forests of banana plants line the edge of the streams, and as we descended the slopes we looked up to behold their lustrous leaves covering large expanses, as though someone had thrown a bright green mantle over the dizzying passes to both beautify and conceal them.

After studying El Chorro in admiration, we continued on our way to the hacienda. It was not long before we saw the estate rising from a furrow cut into the side of the precipice. The roofs of the houses appeared so immediately below the road that it seemed that our steeds would end up treading upon them. Suddenly, the path took a turn and proceeding downhill we soon reached the hacienda, along with the collection of small homes that ringed around it. At the center stood the hacendado's house, the *trapiche*, the barns, the chapel, and an iron latticework that sectioned off the orchard.[25]

The sound of our horses' hooves beating against the stone path brought a servant from the orchard. After extending us a spirited greeting, he took our horses by the bridles and led them to the manger, then returned to the plaza.

"Listen, Juan," my cousin said to him, "this gentleman is my relative, and he'd like to see the orchard."

"Come in, señores."

"Don't we need the administrator's permission?"

"He's in Tequila," Juan answered. "But that doesn't matter. I'm the orchard master. Is this the first time your cousin has come to El Potrero?"

"No," I said, "I've been here a few times before. But that was years ago."

As we spoke, we descended the walkway and entered into a long, wide path with robust orange trees on each side. Behind them we could see a thriving and unrivaled vegetation. We explored that beautiful place in all directions, even its most hidden corners, its groves, even the most isolated and distant. The place was a cross between the Garden of the Hesperides and the Paradise of Adam and Eve.[26] Its fecundity astonished. There, mere plants were trees; trees were colossi. The mameys attained undreamed-of heights; their yellow branches bore huge, stiff leaves and are laden with fruit exceeding even that of the other trees.[27] Mangos rose slender and stately, reaching remarkable sizes. The hacendado had formed a copse of them so dense and beautiful that it provided a broad, living canopy for lunches and outdoor dances. Also lining the banks of the streams were coffee trees laden with those red berries that yield the famous beans; workers have to prop up their limbs so that the latter are not bent and broken by the excess weight. The banana plants form thick forests that wind their way like serpents following the contours of the land, now sinking into deep basins, now rising above the elevations. In this way they resemble some cheerful, tightly regimented army, marching along the slopes in the direction of the water or descending into the sonorous basins that always shimmer with greenery. But the orchard's main attractions were the orange groves that everywhere raised their elegant green crowns, embellished by their white flowers and red fruit. The citrus that hangs in such abundance on its branches peeps through amid a profuse and brilliant foliage.

The fruit of hacienda El Potrero is famous for its outstanding quality. The aromatic banana plants, the enormous and juicy mangos, the avocados, the lime: everything produced here tastes delicious and is fit for a king. The oranges in particular, beautiful to behold and exquisite to smell, are legendary for their scent and sweet flavor. I have sampled the finest oranges of the world—in Cuba, Florida, Andalucia, Africa, Sorrento, Sicily, Jaffe, and Kaiffa—and can truthfully report that those of Potrero hold their own with or even surpass the best of them.

"A lovely place, by my life," I said to my cousin.

"I told you so," he replied. "Knowing your fondness for natural beauty, I was certain that you'd find the journey worthwhile."

"Tequila is without doubt a privileged land!" I continued. "It has beautiful surroundings, while its men are brave as lions, and its women as beautiful as angels, as Guadalajara's celebrated writer Altamirano said a few years ago."[28]

"I'll admit that the surroundings aren't half bad, and Lozada has tested the bravery of the men. But as for the beauty of the women, that's difficult to judge. I challenge you to name one of those beauties."

I kept silent for a moment as I struggled to recall people and names. But I emerged from this difficulty in triumph: "Nieves, the Virgin of La Florida."

"She's not from Tequila," my cousin said with a laugh.

"But she might as well be," I replied.

"Not really, since she doesn't even live in the town. You must confess that what you said about our women is nothing more than rhetoric."[29]

"I would not be so ungallant," I answered, letting out a laugh. "I would give my own life before I did that."

Our guide Juan had come near us and listened attentively to the conversation.

"Do you know Nieves, your mercy?" he asked me.

"That's what I said. Do you know her as well?"

"Not so much. She's my girlfriend."

"Goodness!" I responded. I could not help but stare and ask him, "She's something else, isn't she?"

"Yes, señor," he said, turning red as he hacked away with his machete at the branches that had invaded our path.

Juan was tall, muscular, and fair-complexioned. His slightly pallid skin harmonized with the sweetness of his face, which shone with the honest simplicity of his age and his country upbringing. A near mustache of downy, blond hair barely concealed his upper lip. His eyes were large and melancholy. His smile was peaceful, almost sad. His thick hair, chestnut and almost curly, was unruly but not unattractive. The way that I saw him at that moment, with his pants gathered up to the knees and revealing muscular calves and clean white feet, reminded me of an image that painters like to use as models in paintings of local customs, that is, of Napolitano lads playing the gusla.[30]

No, not a bad couple, I thought to myself. I then continued aloud: "In that case I congratulate you, friend, because the truth is, that girl is really beautiful."

"We would have been marry-fied some time back some time back," said Juan, with all the simplicity of a peasant who opens his heart to the whole world, and who tells his story to the first person who comes along.[31] "And if it wasn't for her young age, and because that old Petra, her aunt, doesn't like me. Nor does that one-eyed Analco."

"And why don't they like you? Is there some reason?"

"I don't know, but I think it must be because I'm poor, because they care about money more than they should."

"Have you two been in love for a long time?"

"Since we were children, even. We are both from Amatitán, and since our families lived next door, we saw each other all day long and played together.[32] No one would have believed that the girl would become so beautiful, because when we were young, she was so ugly that I used to make fun of her by calling her *güera pistoja*.[33] It makes me mad to think about it."

Juan's observation caused me to recall other transformations of this sort that I myself had witnessed. I have known extraordinarily homely girls who upon reaching adolescence experience an astonishing change into beauties. A slow, unperceived, and powerful process takes control of their rough features to perfect them and render them graceful and harmonious. Seeing this metamorphosis has left me puzzled on more than one occasion. How, I asked myself, is this fine, even arrogant, little nose the same flat, upturned nose I used to see? And those wild, rebellious teeth leaning every which way: are they the same string of tiny pearls that shine between those scarlet lips? And those rough, malformed feet: are they the same small feet that Cinderella would have envied? How could an ugly, awkward street urchin end up as this goddess of beauty? And unable to explain a speck of the matter, I remain mute and perplexed; I do not know whether to trace the lines of transformation or simply to enjoy the change as might some blind worshiper of the god Success.

Juan failed to notice the reverie into which I had fallen and instead continued to assail me with the details of his romantic idyll. I listened to a somewhat confused account of the attraction he had little by little come to feel for Nieves, of how she had been kind and amiable to him, almost like a sister, until at last separation had made them recognize their true and reciprocal sentiments. I recall him telling me that he had not employed that sacred formula—"I love you"—in order to make Nieves understand; rather, the two of them by tacit and mutual agreement had made it known that they cared for each other for as long as they could remember. As soon as Juan reached adolescence, he had gone to work with his father. He began as a planter, walking behind a team of oxen that plowed the field and scattering the seeds of corn in the furrows the plow had just opened. Later he became the oxen's driver and eventually moved with his family to this hacienda El Potrero, where he learned the art of tending an orchard, an art his father understood to its fullest. When his father died, Juan took up the position of caring for the orchard. He only saw Nieves on Sunday in the village at mass time, and after mass she would say a few words to him in the marketplace, ignoring the watchful eye of Petra, who was always furious to see him. He suspected Don Santos's louche intentions toward Nieves, and he feared complicity on the part of Petra and Analco in the designs of that perverse hacendado, a man whose immorality and whose abuse of the poor were well known for many leagues around.

"If I had twenty pesos," he told me by way of conclusion, "I would marry her right now."

"But how? Isn't that a bit sudden?"

"I would elope with Nieves, put her up safely in the house of the town cura, and later we would be married. After all, she has no parents, and the *jefe político* would give us the marriage license, even if it infuriated that one-eyed Analco and her aunt."[34]

"To tell the truth, the plan doesn't sound half bad. But twenty pesos would hardly suffice to cover all the costs. The priest's fees alone are that much."[35]

"My plans are all worked out. I would pay the cura ten or twelve pesos and use the rest to buy gifts and finance the wedding."

The hopeful lad laid out his budget and showed me how this amount of money would suffice. He would purchase a rebozo, petticoat, and shoes for Nieves. With the rest he would pay for rice with turkey in *pipián*—the indispensable dish for all weddings—and hire musicians and singers for the dance.[36] I would have found the whole affair depressing had I not seen his eyes so full of joy.

"That's good," I said, my heart now touched. "You go ahead with your plan, and I'll loan you the twenty pesos."

"Truly, señor?" he asked timidly, but with joy.

"Of course," I responded. "But act quickly, because I'm not going to be at Tequila for more than a few weeks."

We explored the terms for repaying the debt, and when at last the meticulous lad was satisfied, he accepted the offer and assured me that as soon as the administrator returned from Tequila, he would ask for leave to go to town and begin preparing things for the plan he had in mind.

Needless to say, from that moment on Juan went overboard in his affection and concern for me, doing all possible to satisfy and pamper. He took us to the orchard's bath, formed by the convergence of two streams, and with blue water of different temperatures. Its bed and banks, both covered by rocks of different sizes and all worn smooth and polished, present a most picturesque sight. Bananas, guayabanas, and lime trees lined its banks and provided a shade beneath which to contemplate that lovely scene. At Juan's invitation and with his kindly provisioning of towels and mats, my cousin and I dipped in to enjoy the indescribable pleasure of contact with that soft, warm, and caressing water. All along the course of its stony channels and dense shade, it produced sounds that were so sweet and so beguiling that I lay back upon the bed of stones and allowed its amorous waves to wash over me. I lay motionless for a long time as I listened in transport to that inimitable music, and, being certain that it was trying to tell me something, I summoned up my spirit to translate its language. But I could not do so, owing to the emotional confusion it awoke within me, emotions of serene happiness but also a sadness that was somehow sweet and yet coupled with vague desires.

As we submerged ourselves in the waters coming from one or the other currents of the confluence, the trees along the banks, shaken by gusts of wind, dropped their mature sweet fruits into that rustic bath that filled us with joy and enchantment. We resembled men from the world's earliest days, as if mortals before us had never come upon this place of amorous secret.

After finishing our bath, we took up our shotguns and enjoyed the pleasures of the hunt, felling the birds that came in flocks to nest in the treetops. Thrush, sparrow, *chachalacas*, parakeets, parrots, and guacamayas succumbed to our fire and dropped to the ground—so many in fact that I grew tired of seeing them lying dead, as much for the beauty of their colorful plumage as out of sorrow for their unfortunate end, which in truth was unjustified.[37] After all, we had no excuse for having injured them, neither on account of some sort of fierce character nor for some delicious meat, since on one hand they were harmless, and on the other unsatisfying as food. It was more to pass the time: a sort of game and target practice, and we kept on shooting at the flock until the birds flew in fear from the orchard to seek out refuge in some overgrown cane field far away.

When it was time to eat, we realized that our idyll was in fact imperfect, because we had quite literally nothing to satisfy our hunger.

"Juan," I said to the orchard master, "do us the favor of fetching some grilled meat, beans, tortillas, and *chile* sauce from one of the huts on the ranchería."

"There's nothing of that sort in El Potrero," he replied crossly. "Didn't the señores bring provisions from Tequila?"

"No, because we thought we'd find something to eat here."

"Señor, here we eat poor folks' food."

"Well, then, what do you live on?"

"Cooked pumpkin."

"Nothing more?"

"Nothing more."

I stood stupefied for a moment, staring at Juan and searching his face for some hint of jest or good humor that might give the lie to his words. But he remained serious, and I had to believe him. To extricate us from this awkward situation, he went off to look for provisions among the hovels nestled within the back country and eventually brought a chicken and some eggs. It was basic, but we managed to improvise a frugal meal that turned out to be better than we would have hoped.

It is authentically shocking to see how campesinos live. They work tirelessly, eat little, go about almost naked, and have no needs or joys beyond those of the animal level. Necessity gives birth to progress: where there are no needs, neither is there incentive, nor improvement, nor a civilized life. Our laborers will rise from the abject condition in which they vegetate the day they aspire to eat better, to dress decently, and to obtain for themselves commodities. When they raise their moral level, so too will rise the Republic.[38]

Despite having subsisted on pumpkins and fruit, Juan showed no signs of being debilitated, a fact that left me utterly surprised; after all, in those days the world had yet to see the famous experiments of Tanner, Suaci, and Merletti, who demonstrated that a man can live for as long as thirty, forty, and even fifty days without eating.[39]

"When you marry Nieves," I told him, "you two will live like Adam and Eve in Paradise."

And given the scant clothing, the vegetable diet, and the beauty of the location, the comparison was rigorously exact.

When the meal ended and the hottest part of the day had passed, my cousin and I commenced our return to Tequila. We said goodbye to Juan, who accompanied us for the better part of the canyon's slope. He promised he would return the visit shortly.

V.

The fiesta that Don Santos proposed to celebrate the blessing of the hacienda's chapel threw Tequila into an unimaginable hubbub. A man of wealth and munificence, he spared no expense in making it the finest possible event, bringing in musicians, preserved foods, and exquisite wines from Guadalajara, all for the purpose of pleasing his guests. These guests came not only from Tequila itself, but also from distant properties and villages, so that the fiesta turned out to be brilliant and overflowing with people. Don Santos was a vain, prodigal man, and for this occasion he threw in all but the kitchen sink, as they say, to create a sensation and to make the whole world speak of his magnificence.

I too was invited, and accompanied by my cousins and the jefe político, I was among the first to arrive at La Florida, which I found all in a stir. The hacendado's plaza overflowed with campesinos. The vaqueros[40] wore leather jackets and vests and rode spirited horses that the former made move in a circle[41] and to gallop in all directions. Some of the servants wandering about on foot lit fireworks that took off with a whistle and exploded high in the air. The guests came in carriages and on horseback, and there were not a few ladies among them. Don Santos followed his own style in welcoming everyone to his home.

"Come in, señores," he said to those who arrived. "Inside, señoritas." Then, "Hey, you," he shouted to a servant, "take care of this gentleman's horse. Are you asleep?" And "Park this carriage under that tree." Finally, he ended by complaining about all the servants, whom he called lazybones, along with certain other terms that do not bear repeating.

The chapel was small, but as it was located at one end of the corridor, those guests who failed to find a seat within instead gathered in the space just outside, a space that, once the door was opened, served as an extension of the tiny chapel itself.

Quite a few ornaments were on display. Green branches were strewn everywhere, along with multicolored streamers, tinsel, and reflecting spheres of white, red, and blue, all hung from the ceiling by slender threads and alternating with golden oranges. These articles made up the altar's main adornments. The cura delivered the blessing and said mass and immediately afterward preached a short sermon. He was a holy man, to be sure, but more gifted in virtue than eloquence. After mass was over, the small bell of the church tower let loose a chime that sounded tired and muffled, as if the bell were made of clay. The music played a loud reveille, and the ensuing fireworks and rifle volleys nearly perforated the guest's eardrums.

Immediately afterward, servants began to circulate trays filled with cups of different wines, and a general libation commenced, something that loosened everyone's tongues and raised the pitch of the voices. The guests invaded the house, spreading out through the corridors, parlor, and private chambers. There was opportunity for a few dances, and soon it was time to eat. Meanwhile, the air filled with the strains of enchanting music, the sound of plates, the tinkling of the wine glasses, and the popping of corks suddenly loosened from their bottles, and everything was voice, animation, and laughter in the enormous, whitewashed basin that substituted for a sitting room.

Around three in the afternoon the fiesta ended, and everyone relocated to the scene of the bullfight. This was a large, four-sided corral surrounded by a broad stone structure with a roof, a structure that led to yet another corral where the hacienda's workers kept and tended to the cattle. Some planks had been placed on the fencing to serve as improvised bleachers. As many guests as could do so settled onto these planks using tule seats.[42] The jefe político and I shared something resembling a box with Don Santos, who was disinclined to separate himself from that official to whom he devoted all his concerns and attentions. Many of the hacendados, and particularly those young sons of rural proprietors who were present, mounted their spirited horses and rode into the plaza, determined to participate in those taurine competitions of skill and luck. The horses looked handsome and their harnesses picturesque. These noble brutes crossed the plaza with their necks arched, ears raised, and heads held high, galloping across the ground in light, graceful steps, like flirtatious women. The riders showed off their jackets of brilliant fabric braided hats with metal fasteners and adornments, with enormous spurs that no conquistador would have disdained, and giant star-shaped wheels with encrusted silver metal plating of the same. The vaqueros crossed the plaza beside their amos. They wore leather clothing and broad palm hats and covered their legs with enormous leather chaps that were tied to the saddle horn. Suddenly, the riders unfastened those brilliantly colored sarapes they wore and waved them in the air in anticipation of the bullfight. Some preferred white, others blue or red, a mixture of colors that made the scene indescribably splendorous.

The rancheros and rancheras who came on foot, and who did not take part in the fiesta, sat on the stone fence, most of them crouched down and covered with their serapes from nose to feet and with their sombreros thrown over their eyes. The more adventuresome of this group let their legs dangle into the corral. The women dressed in clean calico petticoats of different colors and wore high-soled shoes and in some cases lower-cut black shoes or gaudy half-boots. They too cozied up atop the fences, shielding their faces with their rebozos, while the boys climbed to the surrounding treetops, where they shouted and caused a tremendous din generally. This scene played out under a blistering sun that turned the sky into something resembling a sheet of red-hot bronze.

The first contestant was about to enter the plaza when the jefe político said, “There’s still no queen for the bulls, Don Santos.”

“You’re right,” the hacendado answered. “We’ll have to name one. Who would be good for the role?” So saying, he cast an eye over the bleachers where the fair sex was clustered but was seemingly unable to choose among the women there present.

“Whoever you prefer,” said the jefe político, “as long as it’s a beautiful girl, so that the crowd can have some entertainment.”

That suggestion struck a chord in the mind of Don Santos. Turning away from the bleachers, he instead looked to the fence where the campesina girls were sitting, and very shortly a gleam of satisfaction twinkled in his eyes.

"Hey, Pancho!" he shouted to one of the vaqueros. "Go tell that one-eyed Analco that he needs to come to the platform with all his family." Then, turning to us, he added, "Now we've got a queen of the bulls who's worth the trouble."

The vaquero crossed the plaza at a gallop and approached a group huddled under the shade of a mesquite tree. I watched him carefully, and despite some trouble owing to the distance, I managed to recognize Analco, Tía Petra, and Nieves. The vaquero spoke for a moment with Analco and then returned, explaining that the family would soon be coming. And indeed, shortly afterward we saw the aforementioned individuals get down off the fence and approach the platform via the outer part of the plaza. Nieves resisted; she halted every few steps and only kept walking when compelled by harsh words or by discreet shoves on the part of her aunt and Analco.

"What's the matter, Nieves?" asked Don Santos, when we had ascended the platform. "Why are you angry?"

"She didn't want to be here at all, señor," said Petra. "It seems that you aren't the amo."[43]

"She's very rebellious," added Analco with a tone of bad humor, "but you can't give in to her whims."

Nieves remained silent, as was her tendency, and covered her face with her rebozo. She was wearing the red petticoat and blue shoes that appeared to be her only luxuries. Moreover, her hair had been done up nicely, and she sported blue glass earrings and a crimson ribbon on her head. A combination of sun and embarrassment had turned her face so red that she resembled a Castilian rose,[44] and the sour expression on her face, most evident on her lips, gave her that charming grace of an angry child.

"Come on, don't be foolish," Don Santos told her, pointing to a seat at the front of the platform. "Sit here. I've called you to make you queen of the bullfight."

Despite the repugnance she felt, Nieves calmed down somewhat on hearing these words and even seemed pleased. You cannot escape that temptation if you are a young, beautiful ranchera: your age, your vanity, and the tastes of the world in which you live make you listen to these imperious commands of the heart. She still resisted, but only slightly, saying: "No, señor, I'm unworthy of being the queen, with such outstanding señoras present. . . . What would people say if a ranchera were queen? Surely they're going to laugh at me. . . . How can this be, señor? If I'm so ugly and shabbily dressed!" and other similar remarks.

But there was no escaping it: Don Santos, Analco, and Petra forced her to take a seat, or as they say, to be seated on the throne.

"Let's go, girl," Don Santos told her, "you'll be just fine here, next to the jefe político."

"Yes," the jefe added, "don't be afraid. You'll be safe from all harm here."

The jefe político's humorous tone seemed to reassure the poor girl, and slowly she settled into the chair, until at last she looked up to face the crowd in the plaza, carelessly letting the rebozo slip from her face. Analco and Tía Petra remained standing behind her.

The rebellious Nieves having been tamed, Don Santos got up and shouted at the top of his lungs: "The event can begin. Here you have the queen of the bullfight!"

All faces turned to see Nieves, who, caught completely off guard, lowered her eyes and blushed deeply. Men shouted, "Beautiful queen!" The women could barely conceal their disgust over the fact that a mere ranchera should preside over such an important event and should have risen to such a transcendent honor. To its credit, country life lacks that physical separation of classes one finds in the city, and people of all walks of society rub shoulders under the blue canopy of the sky. The amo has the mayordomo and the administrator sit at his table as he dances with their daughters; sometimes he even marries one of them, and if they don't marry, he surely romances—or better said, seduces—them. The female side of the hacendado families are used to these customs and do not react in so passionate a manner as do women of the city. Beyond some murmur of displeasure, or some needling criticism directed at the unfortunate girl, the event neither causes any great uproar nor generates a scandal among the fair sex. Criticisms are expressed pointedly but also with delicacy.

Upon command the vaqueros who had assembled in the adjacent corral worked an immense repertoire of maneuvers with the cattle there to separate the bull that was to enter the plaza. At last, they pried it off from the herd, and the beast entered by the gate, which was subsequently closed by means of sliding bars. The riders and the *toreadores* who walked among them unfurled their brilliant serapes and showed off their cape work with considerable dexterity. The extended cape deceives the animal; believing that it has located its enemy, it charges with its horns held low; the toreador withdraws the cape, stands safely aside, and gives the creature a blow on the head. Unable to control itself, the bull continues its path. In this contest the riders display their abilities, together with the agility of their mounts. It seemed that the bull was about to gore one of those noble horses, when the latter leapt forward to safety, as if impelled by a spring. With their ears raised and nostrils flaring, the horses reared upward, chomping at the bit, their mouths filling with foam, and then walked while turning their heads toward the bull to not lose sight of him and to be able to escape his fury. Some riders became so enthusiastic that they dismounted in order to fight the bull on foot and with spurs on. Each time that someone carried out some maneuver with style and efficiency, a general applause rang out, and the musicians played a reveille. Each fighter was called to the platform of the queen, who with her graceful hands pinned a brightly colored ribbon on the rider's lapel or on his hat or else decorated his chest with a baldric commiserate with the importance of his performance.

The cape work over, the *banderilleros* now began their work. The flags or banderillas hung from a cord suspended between two mesquite trees above the fence. They consisted of brightly colored fabric mixed with tinsel. The bullfighters selected their pennants and waving them they went after the bull in order to stick them in its skin. It was impossible to watch this spectacle without being caught up in the emotion. The fighters no longer carried the capes that had been used to deceive the animal; rather, they carried only the banderillas, incited the bull at close proximity, and, upon turning, fell upon it and dexterously pinned the ribbons upon it. Occasionally one of these fighters fell to the ground. This provoked a murmur of disapproval and some derisive whistles from the spectators. The work of the riders was even more difficult: they had to be extraordinarily talented to manage the banderillas while at the same time escape the bull's horns, for the horses had to come dangerously close to the animal. Very soon the bull's neck was covered with banderillas of different colors. They waved and fluttered on top of its moving hide as the animal ran and charged.

As this was not a contest to the death, once the final act was over the bull was lassoed to ride it. The riders took out their lassos and formed large loops at the end of each one to throw them over the animals. They whirled these lassos horizontally in the air above them, then suddenly hurled them over the animal's head with singular dexterity. Soon the bull's head was bound by two or three ropes that cinched the neck or fell across its face or clutched its horns. The riders quickly wound the ropes around their saddle horns a few times and, positioning their horses as far as possible from the beast, forced them to advance. Other riders seized the bull's tail and, taking advantage of its movements, proceeded to tie up the hind legs. Once they had done so, the riders who had lassoed the head and horns pulled in opposite directions. With the rear legs now raised into the air, the animal could no longer maintain its balance. It wavered for a moment on its front legs, then fell with a blow to the ground, landing on its side with immense force and in the process raising a dust cloud.

It lay there immobile, stretched out over the ground, one of its horns lodged in the dirt, its eyes wide open in desperation, its nostrils flared and panting. With the beast in this condition, the vaqueros rushed up and passed a rope twice around its midsection and cinched it tight. To do so, each time they pulled the rope they had to place their feet on the animal's abdomen, using their legs for greater force. When this improvised harness was sufficiently tight, one man from the group mounted the bull's back and with great effort fastened himself to the ropes that were half-sunk into the animal's sides. He was dressed in leather, with chaps open below the knee to reveal the white pants underneath. He also wore yellow boots, spurs, and a palm hat. As soon as he was satisfied with his position on the bull, the other vaqueros loosened the ropes that bound the neck and hooves so that it could get up; but whether from exhaustion or from the excessive tightness of the harness, the bull remained motionless for a few seconds. Upon seeing this, the rider pricked it a few times with his spurs, while the other vaqueros lashed it with their ropes. The exasperated brute was once again standing, now with its mouth open and frothing, and glaring furiously. Upon sensing the rider on its back, it leapt high into the air and continued to buck powerfully for some distance in the corral. Its dark yellow hide seemed disconnected from its body as it slipped and rocked from side to side. The sheer force of these brute movements shook the rider, who soon lost his hat and was immediately pitched forward so that his brow touched the back of the animal's head, just as his neck struck against the animal's hind quarters, all depending on whether the bull bucked forward or backward. But he stuck to the animal's back, however much the animal, now crazed with fury, did everything possible to shake him off. This struggle raged on for several minutes, until at last the animal began to wear out. At that moment the rider urged it on with shouts or else pricked its flanks with his spurs. The brute once more commenced to buck, only to lapse into a prolonged rest a few minutes later. The vaqueros lashed its haunches with their lariats or stood in front of it using their serapes as capes to execute a few maneuvers. At last, the animal reached such a state of reluctance that it ceased to buck or attack and made no further effort to throw off the rider and, with the vaquero on its back, now trotted about looking for a way to escape from the corral. In view of this, and with the beast now thoroughly tamed, the rider seized the moment to pass under a mesquite tree and, taking hold of its lower branches, lifted himself off the bull and allowed it to pass. A furious applause rang out everywhere, the musicians played a reveille, and two rancheros carried the rider to the queen's platform.

Only at that moment did he reveal his identity. It was Juan, looking elegant and upright in his buckskin clothes.

I cast a glance over at Nieves and saw that she was red as a poppy. She took the most beautiful sash pennant from the collection at her side and placed it over his head and right shoulder, so that it crossed over his chest. As the two of them leaned closer for this ceremony, they said something between themselves and smiled as their faces passed close to each other. Thereafter Juan went away glowing with joy.

However brief the scene, Don Santos did not fail to notice it.

"Well, muchacha," he said to Nieves with a harsh tone of voice, "who is that overgrown monkey?"

"I don't know," she replied, clearly bothered.

"You don't know him?"

"No, señor."

"And the two of you," asked Don Santos, turning to Analco and Petra, who remained standing behind us. "You don't know that bounder? Because that good-for-nothing doesn't come from this hacienda."

"It's been churning in my guts since I saw him, señor amo," said Analco. "Yes, I know him."

"Who is he?" the hacendado continued with a touch of annoyance.

"He's an ill-bred rascal," said Petra, "and he's been at war with us for some time now."

"What for?"

"He's been filling the girl's head with ideas."

"So that's it, is it?" Don Santos asked peevishly. "And he comes here to do the same right under my own nose!"

So saying, he got up.

"Where are you going, Don Santos?" asked the jefe político, who had not paid much attention to the exchange.

"I'm going to fight a bull," he shot back sarcastically.

"But hombre, don't let anything happen to you; leave this matter to the muchachos."[45]

"I'll be back later," he said. "I'm tougher than any muchacho." And with those words he descended the platform and walked off to behind the corral.

Nieves was visibly alarmed.

"What's the matter?" I asked. "Is something wrong?"

"Yes, señor. I'm feeling a pain," she answered with a troubled face.

"Flighty!" Analco growled.

"Are you afraid of Juan?" I asked him cautiously.

Surprised, he turned to look at me, and finding something in my face that calmed him, he kept his lips still, but his eyes told me "yes" in such a way that left no room for doubt.

"This man is the authority here," I said, pointing out the jefe político.

It seemed that my remark settled him down a bit, and he looked away to the plaza.

The bull had by now disappeared, and the riders were unfurling their serapes to begin cape work with another animal. A short distance from us, a ranchero who was sitting on the fence, carried away by the spectacle and perhaps by wine, now let loose a plaintive and monotonous song, tuneless and in a falsetto that resembled those tremulous Oriental songs, paying more attention to what he understood of the lyrics than actually making it beautiful.[46] Thanks to that circumstance, which is common to campesino singing, I managed to listen closely to the words, which ran more or less as follows:

I'll say this and nothing more,
like Havana cedar so fine,
whoever has a beautiful woman
no one has a worse time
and worse if the señorita
is the hot-blooded kind.

The poor man can never have
a woman who's pretty
because a rich man's going to take her
if he doesn't have money
Even if the poor man's right,
he doesn't have any.

The mournful lament of the ranchero had yet to echo when Don Santos reappeared in the plaza, now as a horseman on his dapple-gray colt, a feisty and smartly harnessed animal. The hacendado wore an expression of ill-humor that inspired fear. Without removing the red serape that he had doubled lengthwise, he towered over the beast's haunches, executed a turnaround, carefully taking stock of the faces of those curious onlookers who were sitting on top of the fence. A short distance from where we sat, he abruptly stopped for another bull had yet to appear, and as there was no music nor any great din, we could hear perfectly what he was saying: "Hey, you . . . who are you?"

"Your honor's humble servant," answered Juan (for it was to Juan that he spoke), coming down from the fence with a respectful haste.

"Are you from La Florida?"

"No, señor, I'm from El Potrero."

"What did you come here for?"

"I came for the event, señor amo."

"And who invited you?"

"No one, señor amo. I came because I heard about it."

"You must be a thief. I see that you have the face of a rogue. Get out of here this instant."

"Don't insult me, your honor. I'm a decent man."

"Be careful not to disrespect me, you enormous rogue!"

"No, señor, I'm not disrespecting your honor," said Juan, now whiter than wax and taking off his hat. "The only thing I ask is that you not insult me before so many people."

"Get out, you worthless so-and-so."

"You have no reason to run me off. Have I committed some disorder?"

"Now I'll show you, you scoundrel. So you're not going to go because you're supposedly a good man? Now you'll see."

And following these words, Don Santos, crimson with rage, took out the leather-sheathed sword that hung from his saddle horn and under his left leg, and swinging it furiously struck the young man a stinging blow with the flat of the blade. Juan jumped back as if bitten by a snake and, before anyone had time to think, from God knows where produced an enormous knife. Its burnished blade gleamed threateningly in his hands. But Don Santos was no coward: instead of flinching before the weapon, he seemed to grow more furious still. He burst into a string of horrendous insults, and pricking the horse with his spurs he fell upon Juan. With his knife in his right hand, the imperiled lad took his wide palm hat in his left like a shield and leapt with much agility in order to avoid the blows, waiting for the moment to counterattack. But the combatants made only a few unsteady attempts to land a blow. The plaza quickly filled with people, and twenty strong hands seized and disarmed Juan. Once the vaqueros had him, Don Santos approached and struck the lad's head two or three times with the flat of his sword.

Each blow resounded as it struck against the hardness of the skull. Juan twisted furiously, unleashing a torrent of profanity.

"Hey! Hey!" shouted the jefe político as he leapt from the platform, taking out a pistol that he carried in a leather holster on his waist. "Stop! No fighting here! Control yourself, Don Santos. Don't hit the poor man when he's being held. Let's go. Order here!" And shoving and ordering his way through the throng of people, he at last managed to reach the hacendado.

"This rascal tried to harm me," Don Santos said to the authority. "He deserves to die."

"Calm down, Don Santos. Control yourself."

"Alright," the hacendado answered, "you know that you're the authority here and that for me your word is law." Upon hearing his words, he sheathed the sword once more.

"I understand, my friend. Please do me the favor of stepping back."

"The one who ought to step back is this rogue," the servants shouted to their amo. "Take him to the old barn."

Upon hearing his words, they forcefully laid hands on Juan and carried him away to the barn.

"They're going to put him in the stocks!" cried Nieves, her eyes filled with tears.

I had forgotten all about her. The poor girl was utterly pale, and her chin trembled like that of a traumatized child.

"To the stocks! To the stocks!" shouted Petra. "That's what he deserves."

As for Analco, he had leapt down into the plaza when the whole scene began and was one of the men who seized hold of Juan.

"Don't put him in any stocks," I said. "It's not in Don Santos's power to do that."

Petra said, "He ought to be hacked with a machete. After all, he tried to kill Don Santos."

"Justice can punish him if he's guilty," I insisted, "but Don Santos, no."

Nieves looked at me, her pleading eyes welling with tears.

"Señor," she said to me, "for the love of God, the amo. . . ."

"Don't fear," I said and leapt down into the plaza.

I approached the jefe político and in a few words explained the situation to him. I said that Don Santos was jealous of the young man and in fact was capable of killing him if the lad were left in the hacendado's custody.

"You're right," he told me. "We'll have to take him to Tequila."

"That's a good idea," I replied. "That way we can avoid the hacendado committing some sort of abuse."

We approached Don Santos. The jefe político explained that it was necessary to take Juan away, and that he himself was assuming responsibility for doing so.

"That's not necessary," Don Santos told him. "I'll take charge of giving him what he deserves right here. I need to punish him to set an example for my servants; otherwise, they're going to lose respect for me."

"But since all this happened in my presence," said the jefe político, "I'm obligated to intervene in the matter."[47]

After prolonged debate Don Santos had to yield, albeit very much against his wishes, and he ended by saying: "This rascal requires a severe punishment. I'll present my case before the judge at Tequila."

We headed over to the old barn, an enormous, dilapidated structure that for a time had served as a granary, but that was now creaking and on the point of collapse. There we found Juan with his feet in the stocks. After a prolonged struggle with his captors, he was at last overcome by sheer numbers and had to submit to this torment. Analco was turning the key to the stocks just as we entered. Compelled by the jefe político, he reluctantly reopened the ponderous device and let the victim go free.

These events spoiled the fiesta. For all of Don Santos's efforts to keep it going, he failed utterly. The throng dispersed little by little, and my cousin, the jefe político, and I all took a seat in our carriage and headed for Tequila, with Juan seated next to the driver as prisoner. He was silent and serious, visibly worried and covered with welts. When we reached the town, I told him: "Hombre, Juan, I'm terribly sorry for what happened. What matters now is not to worry about it too much."

"The amo Don Santos abuses poor people," he answered hoarsely. "But I, señor, have a sense of honor and am as much a man as any other."

The reply frightened me, because I realized that it came from a roused and rancorous spirit. I said no more, and we reached Tequila in silence. As I parted ways with the jefe político, I asked him: "What are you going to do with Juan?"

"I'm taking him to jail."

"But what a thing for this poor lad. Couldn't you just make him pay a fine and set him free?"

"No, the matter is serious, because he tried to wound Don Santos."

"But he only acted in self-defense."

"It's a crime of assault and has to go before a judge."

I saw the affair differently than did the jefe político and so said nothing more. Almost without saying goodbye I walked away from the carriage. Because the jail was beside the main plaza and in the direction opposite my house, I could see the jailor escort Juan away as prisoner.[48]

VI.

My grandfather's distillery is a huge construction found on the outskirts of town, on the side opposite from that of the La Tuba gully, so called because this is a place where people throw the *bagazo* from the distilled mezcal, along with rubbish from the taverns.[49] The odors emanating from the stream have a special smell and set the place apart; Tequila smells like *tuba*, just as Atotanilco smells of jasmine.

My cousins kept the business going for a while, although in a smaller scale than in the days of my grandfather. They accompanied me as I paid a visit to the old factory. I explored its interior, pausing every so often to consider, and with no small sadness, the ravages of time and the solitude that reigned everywhere. The patio and corrals were now deserted, although at one time they had been filled with the boisterous bands of muleskinners who carried the liquor to towns throughout the state, and as far away as San Luis Potosí and Zacatecas, points with which my uncle maintained a vibrant commerce. Cribs once overflowing with corn now looked empty and dilapidated; the water troughs, now dry and tumbled down, no longer serviced the multitude of mules and horses that came there to quench their thirst after eating their fill of corn in the mangers. There was none of that crowd of mule drivers who, with their leather harnesses and animal blinders in arm, once bustled about everywhere, taking care of the animals, fastening barrels on their backs, and leading them on with calls, lashes, and whistles. Gone was that incessant activity, that ceaseless coming and going of workers and buyers with which the huge building had once resonated.

My cousins saw that I was a bit melancholy, and they understood what I was thinking, but they limited themselves to telling me, with the tone of an excuse: "What do you want? We're poor, and we do what we can with the business."

I looked over the factory. Of the hundred ovens of earlier days, only eight were now lit. The rest stood silent and abandoned in this vast, dark space with its high ceilings. My cousins still kept up the old method of distilling alcohol, having made no other innovation than introducing two stills of a new system that very few of the local distillers have thus far adopted.

The origins of the mezcal industry lie shrouded in an impenetrable darkness. Did the Tiquiles, that Aztec tribe who inhabited this region before the Conquest, know the secret of converting the plant's sugar into alcohol? No one knows for certain. There are those who insist that they did, although we must wonder why the historians of Nueva Galicia do not say a single word about so important a matter. Nevertheless, to judge from what Mota Padilla writes in Chapter 65 of his respected history, it seems that the industry does predate the Conquest, since he compares mezcal wine with *tepachi* and *tejuino*, both of which are definitely indigenous beverages.[50]

The inhabitants of Tequila will mention a fact known by tradition, namely, that the production of tequila began in the town of Amatitán, which lies six leagues away in the direction of Guadalajara. They further report that the Amatitecans were those who invented the methods of cooking, pressing, fermenting, and distilling the mezcal. The industry eventually passed from there to Tequila. This latter town had attained a greater level of development, came to dominate distilling, and even gave its name to the product. I cannot vouch for these accounts and merely repeat the matter as it was told to me. But if I were to express an opinion, I would have to say that the tequila process is partly indigenous, partly colonial. I believe that the native peoples would surely have discovered the existence of sugars in the plant by reason of their close contact with nature, because even today we use the indigenously derived word *tatemar* to refer to the act of cooking the plant's heart, which in reality is an enormous vertical root. This word's indigenous etymology indicates that the Indians performed said operation. Likely the Indians cooked, pressed, fermented, and drank mezcal without distilling it. They were thus able to become intoxicated, although without the intensity of effect that comes with distilled liquor. Then the Europeans arrived and, astonished by the quantity of sugar contained in the agave heart, properly *tatemado*, together with its agreeable taste, conceived the idea of distilling the fermented product by use of fire. In this way they managed to produce a spirited beverage that with the passage of time achieved great popularity and widespread consumption, to the point of winning a gold medal at the Paris exposition.[51]

My cousins employed the old method in their factory. After digging a colossal pit in the ground, they line its walls by piling large stones on top of one another, without the use of cement. This is the oven. To cook the mezcal, they light a pyramid of firewood in the middle, then place the agave hearts around it in symmetrical fashion, until they reach the level of the surface. At that point the oven is covered over with moist dirt, although allowing the fire a breathing hole at the top. After several days, when the wood is completely consumed, the oven is covered and the cooked mezcal, or *tatemado*, is removed. The white interior has now changed to a dark yellow. In this condition it is easy to tear off the fibrous leaves, or *pencas*, leaving exposed the juicy heart of the plant. Its liquid is perfumed honey and possesses a most pleasing flavor.[52]

There is no need to point out that this process is both primitive and fraught with problems. The juice that drips from the cooked pencas falls upon the walls of the oven, where much of it is absorbed, and at considerable loss to the distillers. Nevertheless, those same distillers insist that any other method robs the mezcal of its unique fragrance. True or not, the distillers unanimously believe it, and in regard to the ovens, they practice and perpetuate the ways of the Tiquiles.

Once the mezcal is cooked, it is taken to the *tahona*, a heavy circular stone in the shape of a wheel, which in turn rotates around an axis.

A team of oxen are used for moving this apparatus. The wheel, the oxen, and the driver (working barefoot and with pants knee-high) roll over the mezcal repeatedly. Once pressed in this manner, it yields all its mezcal, which soon fills the tahona. Without bothering to separate the bagazo, the workers then collect that juice in large buckets that empty into enormous cylinders. Fermentation takes places within a few days. The must[53] is extracted and then poured into vats built into thick masonry benches and used for distilling alcohol. Underneath the cylinders are wood-fired ovens. As the must boils, its alcoholic portion evaporates and subsequently recondenses onto the surface of the bottom of an iron or copper receptacle kept constantly cold by means of water poured onto the top. In this way the distiller manages to capture the spiritous vapor as it condenses, and the liquid alcohol runs via a canal fixed to an opening in the metal vessel. The liquid so obtained is the famous aguardiente of Tequila. When lukewarm it is sweet and does not burn the mouth. It is highly intoxicating and is called *tuba.*[54]

I was absorbed in these details when, upon reaching the dark end of the distillery, I heard a woman's voice calling my name.

"Señor, señor," the voice said.

"Who's calling me?" I asked.

"It's me," replied the unknown woman as she approached.

It was Nieves, so wrapped in her rebozo that her bewitching eyes could scarcely be seen beneath its thick folds. Her appearance caught me by surprise.

"What's the matter?" I asked.

"Señor," she answered, "I've run away from home."

"How could that be?"

"That's exactly what I've come to explain to Your Mercy so that he can advise me."[55]

"Very well, Nieves. I'm listening."

"Since yesterday I've been in Tequila, put up in the home of someone I know. The truth is that the day before yesterday, the day of the fiesta at La Florida, many things happened after you left, things so horrible that I don't know how to tell you about them."

Indeed, the poor girl's voice was trembling and excited.

"I sought you out because I have seen your concern for the poor. As I was saying, the day before yesterday, after you left for Tequila, some truly terrible things happened. Tía Petra, Don Cruz, and I went home to our shack, and they beat me so severely for what happened with Juan that I cried and cried. I tried to leave the shack, but Don Cruz and my tía wouldn't allow it. Don Santos talked about nothing but what a bandit Juan was, and how he was going to be sent before the judge, and that he wanted to see him shot. I could only cry and keep quiet. As all of this was going on, it got very late. Everyone had gone home and there was no noise at all in the hacienda, except for the dogs barking. Don Santos took out his watch, saw that it was late, and told me that it was time to go to sleep. He whispered a few words to Don Cruz, who answered him in the same tone, and after their short conversation Don Cruz got up and called my tía to go outside the shack. I thought they would come back right away, but time passed, and no one returned, so I went to the door to leave. Don Santos sat close beside me on the tapextle, so I made for the door to leave. When he saw I was getting up he grabbed me by the arm to stop me.

"'Where are you going?' he asked.

"'I'm going to look for my tía.'

"'She'll be back directly; wait for her.'

"'I'll come back,' I said as I managed to free myself. 'Let me go.'

"'No, little Nieves. Stay here with me. Don't you want me to keep you company?'

"'No, señor.'

"'Are you afraid of me?'

"'I don't know!'

"So I kept trying to leave, and the amo kept holding me back. Little by little we both tried all the harder until at last we were struggling with all our might. When I saw that I could not free myself from his clutches, I shouted at the top of my lungs: 'Tía! Tía!'

"No one came to my call. My voice was lost in the silence and darkness of the night, and only the neighbors' dogs, roused by my cries, barked with more force. Now trying to cause alarm however I could, I began to shout:

"'Thieves! Neighbors! Thieves!'

"It was all in vain. Later I found out that several persons did come to help me, but that my tía and Don Cruz, who were watching over the shack the whole time, one on each side, reassured them and sent them away, telling them that I had been punished for something I did, and that was why I was shouting.

"Meanwhile, our struggle continued. It was a horrible scene. The tallow candle that was on the table fell over in all the violence, and the shack went completely dark. I defended myself as best I could and resisted as much as my strength permitted. I felt the sweat run down my forehead, my heart beating as if it wanted to jump out of my mouth; I could barely breathe. My new skirts and blouse were torn: every time I fell or tried to get up, I could hear the fabric tearing. At first Don Santos laughed. After that he turned serious and began to curse me. I went from fear to indignation, and from indignation to rage. My fists struck his face and tore out the hair of his beard, and he hit me and kicked me. I didn't even feel the blows because I was furious. Finally, Don Santos tired and said to me: 'Now you'll see, you wretched girl, how I deal with your defiance!'

"A moment later I realized that he had something hard in his right hand: it was pistol. I thought that he was going to shoot me, but the worst he did was hit me with the barrel. At that point I could no longer struggle. I stepped back, defending myself with my hands and in that way absorbing the pain and cruel injuries. Eventually he managed to land a hard blow over my head, and I fell to the ground. I thought I was done for, but I recovered right away. Don Santos seized me by the arms and held me there lying on the floor. But by accident in the darkness, I managed to find the hand that held the pistol. I grabbed it and bit down so fiercely that he was forced to let go of the weapon. As soon as I had it in my hand, I thrashed wildly, hitting him repeatedly and hard, wherever I could. I think that I managed to strike his face, because I aimed high and felt that the pistol barrel struck something soft. In that way I got free from my aggressor. Taking advantage of the moment, I opened the door and fled from the shack. Since the night wasn't as dark as the inside of the shack, at a distance I could see my tía without her seeing me. I jumped over the fence and hid in the underbrush, and with the aid of the most Holy Virgin I headed for the town. It was midnight when I reached this house. Its owner was kind enough to let me in, to treat my wounds, and to lend me some clothes."

So saying, Nieves showed me the large welts that seared her face, arms, and hands. A rabid indignation came over me. I know of nothing worse than a man who raises his hand to strike a woman, nor is there anyone more savage than the man who injures a woman struggling to defend her honor. The amo who bribes a family in order to force himself upon a poor girl; the old woman who betrays her own blood in hopes of filthy lucre; the shameless villain who becomes procurer for lascivious old men: what name do they deserve? What punishment would not be merited? Fruit ripe for the gallows, and how refreshing it would be to see you dangling in the air!

"Wretches!" I managed to say as I clinched my fists.

"Señor," Nieves continued, "I'm afraid that my tía, Don Cruz, and the amo will come to Tequila and carry me back to the rancho. The lady of the house where I'm staying told me that she thought she saw Don Cruz in the plaza this morning."

"You're right: there is danger here."

"They won't respect the sanctity of the home. If they come looking for me, they'll force their way in and take me away, whatever scandal it may cause. Please be so kind as to hide me in a safe place where they don't dare to enter."

"I have an idea," I told her after a pause. "I'll take you to the cura's house."

"Wherever you may think fit."

"Let's go without wasting another minute."

On the pretext of seeing to some business matters I said goodbye to my cousins.

"That's good business, I swear," said one of them as he cast a malicious glance at Nieves.

Conscious of the need to save time, I said nothing and headed out.

After hearing my account, the kindly cura was only too happy to offer his home for so humanitarian an end. He only imposed one condition: that I say nothing to anyone about the matter, so that he not become the victim of some devilment. Since this was exactly what the poor girl and I had in mind from the beginning, we only too happily agreed. In this way she came to live in the cura's house, and I went away satisfied at the small service I had rendered to a young woman so persecuted and abandoned.

VII.

Four days after the events just described, the judge summoned me to make a deposition regarding the events at La Florida. My interview with the judge was more friendly than official. I explained to him, clearly and in full detail, all that I had witnessed.

"This is not what appears in the transcripts of the investigation," he told me.

"That's strange," I replied, "because the events in question happened in front of quite a few people, and they happened exactly as I described."

The judge continued: "The owner of the hacienda has lodged an accusation."

And indeed, I then saw the declaration that Don Santos had presented to the judge, a document in which he accused Juan of attempted homicide.

"And is there someone who supports this monstrous lie?"

"Yes, señor. Various witnesses attest to its veracity."

"And among those, I suppose, are in all probability a one-eyed man and a red-haired old lady?" I exclaimed sarcastically.

The judge said nothing, but from the expression on his face I could see that I had struck home.

"Don Santos," I murmured, "you ought to be called Don Diablos."

"Why?" the magistrate said with a laugh.

"Because his name contrasts so sharply with his nature; he's a scheming and perverted man."

Bewildered, the magistrate stared at me. Only someone who had seen the situation could have an idea of the enormous prestige that surrounds the names of the rich in small towns. Hacendados are accustomed to being grand, all-encompassing powers who do and undo according to their whims in matters of town affairs; the *ayuntamiento*,[56] the political authorities, even the judges themselves respect them, fear them, and always try to mollify them. This does not mean love; at the very least they abhor the hacendados, but they carefully conceal that hatred in order not to stir up ill will. Don Santos was one of those rich individuals generally detested for his arrogance, for his ill manners, for his dominating character; but in the village, there was no one who dared to confront him. Everyone spoke under their breath, but they managed to keep him happy in order to avoid retaliation.

Yes, indeed, I said to myself, Don Santos does have a perverted character. I say as much because I have seen it. And I went on to recount to the magistrate, in utmost detail, everything I knew about Don Santos and his intended advances toward Nieves.

"It doesn't surprise me that you come to me," the magistrate replied, casting a glance at his office's door to assure that there was no one was listening. "I've often heard rumors of that sort concerning the man in question."

"And why have you done nothing?"

"Because no one has dared to testify before me regarding his misconduct. They whisper in private, but no one will stand before the court of justice. Regarding the episode you mention, for example, you are the first who has come to state what he knows of the matter."

"It's for that reason, then, that Juan has no hope of release from jail. . . ."

"Perhaps not; yesterday he was declared imprisoned on legitimate grounds."

"That's a miscarriage of justice."

"That could be. But I have to respond to testimony, and of those who have appeared before me, no one has given grounds to pursue the investigation."

"Perhaps you're right. But it would be good not to interview only those persons suggested by the accuser. Summon other, more impartial witnesses to the court. What does the jefe político have to say?"

"Have you seen the statement he sent to me regarding reasons for the arrest?"

I read the document with much surprise. It stated that Juan, rebuked by the hacendado, had tried to stab him with a knife and in the presence of numerous witnesses. But it said nothing of the circumstances surrounding the event.

"This is incredible," I murmured, flabbergasted. "This lad is being sacrificed. May God have pity on him."

I imagined the fate that awaited him, and in my mind's eye I saw the terrible picture that was his future. Condemned to suffer for years in prison, sent to Guadalajara in the company of hardened criminals; locked away in the penitentiary along with his anger, his resentments, and the depraved company of the other prisoners;[57] corrupted by hatred, by rage, and by desperation; turned to wickedness like the others, and with the completion of his sentence returned to society, driven by ferocious passions and a thirst for vengeance—this is what I imagined in those brief moments of silence.

"I have informed you of the truth," I said as I rose. "You will do what you think necessary so that it may figure into the investigation, with the knowledge that the prisoner is innocent of these criminal accusations."

"I promise that I will do all possible to assure justice," the judge replied, offering me his hand. But his face betrayed his worried mind.

I left the magistrate's office more surprised and troubled than ever by what appeared the probable course of events.

VIII.

In those days there was a revolution afoot in the country, one of those struggles that unfortunately are all too common in our history. A military officer had risen against the existing government and had embraced various causes in order to dazzle the gullible. The old tendency to pronouncements and uprisings that only recently had gone into remission now returned once more.[58] Guerrillas mounted their horses for battle and again took up their rusting arms. Bandits came out of their dens on the pretext of defending public ideals, and very quickly the Republic was filled with alarm, with our interests both at home and abroad severely threatened.

There had been talk in Tequila of raids on the part of some rebel bands, but nothing was known for certain, and so no one was worried about the revolution, as if it were something happening on the other side of the ocean.

Meanwhile, I continued the life of a tourist, enthusiastically contemplating and enjoying the beauty of nature.

To the west of Tequila runs a stream that descends from the slopes and laps at the foothills. The clear and refreshing waters of the Atiscua River come down through the exuberant vegetation of the ravines, power the mills that line its edges, wind their way away from the town, and at last tumble into the depths of La Barranca. I was in the habit of mounting my horse at daybreak and riding along the banks of the stream to a distant point along the banks, where massive trees alternating with rocky terrain offer shade favorable to the fascinated traveler. The adjacent lands, covered with bananas and cane breaks, enliven the journey with their soft, green color, while flocks of birds peep and warble amid the foliage in the remotest and most isolated places. Tormented by the rugged nature of its bed, the stream goes tumbling and frothing with a sustained monotonous murmur. I went to this pool each day to take a bath. As I entered the water, I left my horse tethered to a rock or a tree limb; when the first rays of golden sunshine shimmered on the moving surface of the water, they found me in the middle of the stream, intoxicated by the scene's ineffable charm.

As I was returning from the Atiscua one morning, I was surprised by an unusual movement that I observed on the outskirts of town. In the streets that led from the center to the outskirts I could see passers-by forming into groups, and to judge from their appearance their conversation was alarming. I approached one of them and asked him:

"Could you please tell me what this uproar is all about?"

"What!" he exclaimed. "Then you must be blind. It's a pronunciamiento."

"But where is it? I can't seem to make out what's happening."

"Look, there they go," he answered, pointing a finger.

I glanced toward the direction he indicated and saw some riders at the end of a long street, racing toward the center of town. Without bothering to thank the man, I continued on. Upon reaching the plaza, I witnessed a fast-moving scene that I had little time to analyze. The riders whom I had previously seen from afar entered like lightning bolts, reached the jail, then abruptly halted. They came with rifles in hand. I vaguely realized that this was an assault.

"Viva México!" shouted the leader of the riders. "Surrender, *desgraciados!*"[59] And so saying, he and his companions pointed their weapons at the pale and surprised soldiers who made up the guard. The sentinel tried to resist, but he received a shot at point-blank range, one that removed him completely from the struggle. His fellow guard members made no further effort to defend themselves.[60] They handed over their rifles and were now reduced to trembling with fear under the watchful eyes of the riders, while others of this latter band dismounted and walked with determination into the jail. The captain of the guard had been caught unawares by the attack and had tried to escape . . . but to no avail. A few moments later he reappeared at the door of the jail, beside himself with rage, accompanied by two of the pronunciados. Deprived of his pistol, he went to join his own defenseless soldiers.

While all of this was happening on one side of the plaza, a second group of mounted men had reached the other side, where they halted before the door of the jefe político, right next to my own home. There was no guard here and no possibility of resistance. The jefe político had also tried to hide, or to jump over the adobe walls of his patio, but very quickly he was caught by the bloodhounds sent to find him. Having stopped at the door of my house in order to see where all of this was going to end, I caught sight of the jefe in his portico, his expression startled and angry.

Shortly afterward the guerrilla chieftain arrived. He was an old revolutionary and well accustomed to these sorts of dramatic turns: one of those men who might set out with his soldiers at a moment least expected, headed for destinations unknown, and arrive at a place where no one was expecting him, and from a point of origin equally mysterious.[61] Two leagues from Guadalajara, he had issued the cry of revolt in some shabby village and without stopping had headed straight for Tequila. The picket of soldiers who guarded the roads had changed sides and joined his forces, leaving the routes of public transportation abandoned to the mercy of evildoers. By the time he reached the town he commanded some sixty men, armed and mounted. Almost all were dressed like rancheros, but among them one could also see a few with tattered shirts and white cotton trousers, mounted on wretched horses of skin and bone, and here and there a soldier wearing the uniform of the state's public security forces and riding a fine military steed.

The chieftain was noticeable among other things for the proud animal he rode, dark chestnut, tall, powerful, and full of spirit; by the flannel suit he wore; by the bright, braided hat that covered his head; by the thick folds at the back of his neck; by the stout yellow leather boots that could be seen when he raised his waterproof chaps; and by the pistol and dagger, adorned with lace and silk tassels, that he wore on his belt in calfskin leather sheathes embroidered with silver thread. Approaching the jefe político, he extended a hand without dismounting and said in a friendly tone: "Good morning, amo. How long has it been since you expected a visit from me?"

"Good morning," replied the jefe político rather dryly. "What do you want?"

"Not much," the rebel chieftain responded. "We need some money for a journey, and we come to see if you wouldn't be kind enough to give it to us. But if you won't give it to us willingly, we'll take it by force."

"We've been taken by surprise, and you're giving the orders here."

"That's right, amo," the captain chortled. "We got up earlier than you, but all the better, because that way we can avoid something regrettable."

In reality, the rebel leader was not a hard fellow to get on with. He enjoyed a certain good-naturedness, one tinged with a ranchero's cunning and the ironic streak of a braggart. Encouraged by his character, the jefe político gradually calmed down, and the two men began to converse.

My aunt knew nothing of this episode, so quickly and quietly had it all happened. I told her about it, and she was filled with terror for her children, who were not home at that moment. But one by one they returned from the countryside, and she was relieved to see them safe and sound. And in truth, no one had been bothered in any way. The whole world was passing through the streets, and aside from the change of government (that is, the momentarily indisposed government), everything went on as normal.

I ate breakfast hastily, and not without a churning of emotion, and thereafter I went to the window to see how things were going. The pronunciados had dispersed in all directions and were fraternizing with the townsfolk. Some were having their own breakfast, in this case milk with pumpkin and flame-broiled camote; others drank tequila in the stores.[62] Everyone went about relaxed; they forgot all about the rifles that stood on the floor or hung on the wall racks, and at the same time seemed reconciled to being the victims of this coup attempt, as much as had there been a different group much like their own, angry and determined, that competed with them.

Shortly afterward I was not a little surprised to see a number of peace-abiding citizens among the band of rebels, men such as the most accomplished shoemaker of the town, as well as a *huizachero*, or shyster lawyer, who made a living pestering the magistrates with his legal puzzles. Now armed, these honorable citizens crossed the plaza, decrying the government and spewing out a revolutionary plan that served as a pretext for this uprising.

Meanwhile, the jefe político, deprived of his supreme authority in the town, had fallen to the position of mediator between the inhabitants and the triumphant chieftain. This latter individual wished to impose a tax of 3,000 pesos, but in response to the entreaties of the jefe político, he agreed to cut that amount in half. The most prominent citizens of the town were convened for the purpose of informing them of this decision and so that they could assemble the "forced loan" in the manner they saw fit.

One of my cousins was called to this junta and a short time later he returned, explaining that his household would have to contribute 200 pesos, a sum that did not seem all that exaggerated under the circumstances. But since my aunt did not have metal currency on hand, the urgency of the situation made it necessary to sell a young bull at a mere fraction of market price.

While the junta was underway, another singular but quite representative scene was underway. By order of their chieftain, the revolutionaries had liberated all the jail's prisoners, hardened criminals as well as those jailed for some minor infraction. The liberated men received the customary invitation to join the revolutionary cause, to which they agreed in unison, affirming themselves stout-hearted supporters of the political plan that was to save the nation and simultaneously crying death to the existing government. Following a general roundup of arms and horses in all the homes, the former prisoners now rode in broad daylight and mounted with joy and victory written on their faces.

Since the time of Padre Hidalgo, most rebel chieftains have filled out their ranks using this same method.[63] The conduct of the Father of Independence can be excused by reason of his extraordinary circumstances, but one cannot ignore the pernicious precedent he set, one that all subsequent revolutionaries have followed.

Luckily, this time the freeing of prisoners had one positive effect among all the unfortunate ones, and that was the liberation of the hapless Juan, who was facing the prospect of a lengthy trial and even lengthier prison term. Indeed, the orchard keeper now saw the bright sunshine and breathed the open air of the street at a moment when he least expected to do so. He suddenly found himself armed and converted into a paladin of a political cause. He must have felt dumbfounded at first, but he accepted the circumstances as they came, chose his course without hesitation, and was soon to be seen trotting across the plaza on the back of a valuable horse formerly property of one of the wealthier inhabitants, a man who could only bemoan the terrible loss to his stables.

Upon seeing me Juan halted and approached my window.

"May God grant Your Mercy a fine morning," he said to me, doffing his hat.

"Good morning, Juan," I replied.

"Here Your Mercy sees me a free man," he continued, breathing heavily as though to take in the whole atmosphere of the moment.

"God be praised. Accept my congratulations."

"I truly deserve them. It seems that if it weren't for the pronunciamiento, they would have left me to rot in jail or would have shotted me."[64]

He smiled bitterly, then continued.

"What do you hear from La Florida?"

"Nothing," I told him. "The only thing I know is that Nieves is here."

"With her tía and the one-eyed fellow?"

"No, alone. She's at the cura's house."

"God be praised! But does Your Mercy know how this happened?"

"Yes," I told him. "I took her there myself. Fed up with her family, she came to this town and asked me to put her up in some safe location."

"A thousand thanks to Your Mercy. There can be no doubt that those wretches must have given her a thrashing, and for that reason she has fled."

"Perhaps."

"It's me they ought to thrash, and not that poor girl. And what of Don Santos?"

"I've heard nothing about him."

"You can't imagine how badly I want to catch up with him over there. Now we can settle things man-to-man, and not with me tied up, the way he caught me the other day."

"Are you still thinking about that?"

"How am I *not* going to think about it? I'll remember it for the rest of my life."

"Past is past. You're a free man now, and you ought to let it go."

"Absolutely not!" Juan replied, raising his voice and making a furious gesture. "That amo Don Santos is going to have to pay."

It was in vain that I tried to dissuade him from his plans for vengeance: I saw that I could not change his mind, so instead I tried to change the conversation.

"And now," I asked, "what are you thinking of doing?"

"Follow the revolution, what else? I can't live here; if I stay, they'll put me back in jail."

"Probably."

"Well, forward, then, and we'll see what happens!"

"Alright," I told him jokingly, "what is this cause that you're going to defend?"

"I don't know."

"Why are you taking up arms?"

"I don't know that, either."

"Who is this general to whom you're shouting *vivas?*"

"Who knows what mother he came from?"[65]

"Then you're a pronunciado of considerable importance."

"They only thing I know is that I've pronounced for my own liberty and against despotism."

"You've hit the nail on the head: it so happens that what you've just said is a political program in itself."

"Don't laugh, amo. You've already seen that I'm a hard-working, peace-abiding man, and that I'm joining this band because I've been forced into it."

"I know that, Juan, and don't take my jokes too seriously. Has getting armed and mounted made you testy?"

"Your Mercy's in a mood for jokes today, and you can use them with me. I'll be back later."

And suddenly interrupting the conversation, he galloped away on his fine horse. He was undoubtedly headed to the cura's house, because the priest later told me that an hour after this conversation took place, a mounted pronunciado had entered the pórtico of his home, asking for him. Fearing some catastrophe, the cura's first instinct was to hide.

"Where is the señor cura?" the unknown rider asked.

"He's not at home," the servants replied.

"Tell him not to be afraid," the rider continued, "and that I've not come to do him harm."

"He's not at home," the servants repeated.

"The truth is that I don't care whether he's at home or not; the person I want to talk to is the girl who was left here."

Upon hearing these words, the cura came out of the bedroom where he was hiding and approached to speak with the pronunciado.

"How can I help you?"

"How is Your Mercy's health?"

"Well. And what may I do for you?"

"Your Mercy need fear no injury. I want nothing of you. The only thing I need is to talk with the girl who was left here."

"What girl?"

"The girl Your Mercy has in his good house."

"No girl has been left here. Who told you such a lie?"

"The person who told me is no liar."

At that point Juan explained to the cura what I had told him.

"Supposing all of this is true, I still cannot permit what you are asking."

"It's not out of bad intentions, señor cura."

When saying this the priest trembled, almost unable to speak, and visibly filled with terror.

"May Your Mercy think carefully. I mean no harm to your house and only want to speak with the girl."

"I can't allow it."

"I'll do it, right or wrong."

"Do whatever you want."

"If that's the case, then Your Mercy is to blame if I push you aside."

So saying, Juan dismounted from his horse and made for the elderly priest with a headful of steam. Stunned and bewildered, the cura fled to the safety of a room that opened to the corridor. As the key was hanging out of the lock, Juan gave it a turn and then placed it in his pocket, essentially leaving the priest sequestered within. Immediately thereafter, Juan, with his hand on his pistol, addressed the gaggle of servants, which consisted of various women and an Indian errand boy.

"Let's go," he told them. "Take me to the girl."

The servants, frightened out of their wits but loyal to the end, remained silent. To overcome their resistance Juan saw it necessary to give the Indian a few light blows with his pistol.

"You'll see that I can make you talk," he thundered.

"Don't kill me, Your Mercy," said the terrified Indian.

"Take me to where she is, or I'll beat the living daylights out of you."

"Follow me, Your Mercy."

And the frightened Indian boy led Juan to the back of a large corral, where the kitchen was located.

A few moments later, the revolutionary left the curate in the company of Nieves. He placed her on the saddle of his horse, then sat on the rump behind her and headed out with his precious treasure.

The news of this event saddened me, because in no small part I was to blame for what happened, for the simple fact of having been sufficiently imprudent to tell Juan where Nieves was hiding. My sorrow was all the more when I learned that the ardent young lover, doubtless from mere forgetfulness, had carried off the key to the room in which the poor cura was shut away and that the priest had spent difficult hours in that jail cell, because no one had been able to locate a blacksmith to open the door as quickly as might have been desired.

It was probably three in the afternoon when the pronunciados, having eaten and rested, at last received their "loan" and concluded their roundup of arms and horses, saddled up, and rode out of town. They were all well mounted and armed and totaled more than a hundred in number, thanks to the prisoners and sympathizers they found in Tequila.

As the group paraded out of the plaza, I was surprised to see a woman among the riders. She rode the horse of yet another wealthy inhabitant. The animal was luxuriously harnessed, the saddle doubtless belonging to the owner's wife. This female rider concealed her face behind an enormous white kerchief that covered her forehead, nose, and mouth, leaving only her eyes visible. This same woman wore a wide-brimmed palm hat against the sun, and she wrapped her torso in a highly colored rebozo of fine cloth. I studied her eyes and realized that I recognized her, not so much by her invisible face, but rather by her proximity to Juan, who rode next to her: she was Nieves. Both halted, then came close to the window to say goodbye.

"We'll meet again, señor amo," Juan said to me as he stretched out his hand.

"Adios, Juan. Best of luck."

"Adios, señor," Nieves said timidly, blushing.[66]

"So, you two are leaving now?"

"What else can we do, señor amo? Wouldn't you do the same if you were in our place?"

I laughed.

"Perhaps," I said.

"My only regret," Juan continued, "is not settling scores with the amo Don Santos."

"He probably went to Guadalajara."

"Don't worry. He probably still hasn't recovered from the pistol-whipping Nieves gave him."

His response startled me. There was no doubt: the girl had told him everything that happened.

"That could be," I told him. "And if it is, then Nieves took revenge with her own hand."

"The best is yet to come," Juan replied with rancor in his voice.

"Mine is still coming."

The crowd passed, and the two of them hastily said goodbye in order to catch up. Upon seeing them leave, I fell into a deep reverie thinking about the curiosity of human destinies. Given her age, her inclination, and her natural timidity, Nieves seemed to have been born to use her talents in the tranquility of the home and in the isolation of a happy anonymity. And events might have pushed her to extremes that she, left to her own devices, could not have endured, as happened when she had to use her own personal strength to save herself from dishonor. As it was, she now had to commit herself to the fortunes of an illicit union in the middle of an uprising.

Juan, for his part, would have gone on living happily in that tiny paradise that he tended, taking care of the plants and fruits like the hermits of old, and would never have left that place, nor would he have ceased to be a timid and innocent lad, had it not been for the misfortune that a seducer had inflicted on his promised bride. He had now become a man of war and bore within him a heart filled with rage and hatred. In a mere moment the pathos of their existence had turned inside out.

Owing to blows from without they had suffered an unanticipated change of fortune; their star had shown peacefully on the horizon, and suddenly it glowed blood red and threatening.

The unfathomable mystery of human life! I do not believe that man is the plaything of factors that, however powerful he may be, force him to descend from the lofty pedestal where he, a free and intelligent being, has been placed by his nature. But I do believe that while retaining his fundamental free will through all the vicissitudes of the world, he may receive from the outside world irresistible pressures that compel him to change roles, through a fortuitous turn of events prepared by some unseen hand.

IX.

"A conejo ido, pedradas al matorral" goes the refrain: "Throw stones at the brush once the rabbit has already gone."

The revolutionaries had scarcely left town when the jefe político and the captain of the guard, who in truth had suffered no harm, rediscovered their former spirits and, hoping to recover their prestige through a belated show of force, now authorized measures for the town's defense. After searching for a while, they managed to locate some rifles that the residents had kept out of the pronunciados' hands. With these they armed the guards, and dividing the men into three small groups, they stationed one in the church tower, one on the terrace roof of the jail, and one in the jefe político's office. Not content with these measures, the individual to whom the government had entrusted the sacred charge of authority called together a highly select group of residents and exhorted them to take up arms themselves to prevent those vandalic hordes from invading the town yet again.

"It's a shame," the jefe politico said, "that the same town that knew how to bravely resist Lozada and his savage bands should have been taken so easily by a guerrilla band so small and so disorganized. I'm hoping for this town's famous courage to prepare to forcefully repel another attempt on the part of those vandalistic revolutionary mobs."[67]

One of those in attendance then voiced an objection:

"There's no shame on the part of the residents. The only shame here rests on the authorities who were supposed to keep the peace. We did our part by paying the taxes that the government demands, and those taxes are nothing to sneeze at. It's the state authority here who's supposed to be keeping order and security here. We fought against Lozada because his army threatened us with destruction and barbarism, but not because we wanted to become the permanent defense of some political cause. The truth is that we don't particularly care if it's Pedro or Juan who governs, as long as that person can hold up his end, and we have no desire to risk taking a bullet to defend the government. Let it defend itself . . . if it can."

In any other circumstance the jefe político, impetuous man that he was, would have been overcome with rage to hear such talk. But since he was still humiliated by what had happened, he pretended to pay no attention to this combative response and limited himself to asking, in as ingratiating a way as possible, for the help of these honored gentlemen in organizing a common defense. There is no doubt that any affront to authority results in a loss of prestige, not only because those who witness these affronts see themselves as the injured parties and become defiant, but also because the authority himself loses his power, respectability, and self-confidence!

Fortunately, there were people with good sense who came forward to mediate the argument, and it was agreed upon by the majority of those present to lend the jefe político a hand in placing the town in a state of readiness.

When night came the residents shut themselves up in their homes early. No streetlamps were lit, no stores remained open. Nor was there the normal petty commerce, the marketplace lit by the flames of *ocote*-resin torches.[68] When the great bell of the tower sounded the curfew, it sounded gloomy and fearful, the herald of public mourning and terrifying risk. As I sat by my window, I saw the plaza dark and empty, with not so much as a sound to ruffle the unnerving silence. Houses loomed in the shadowy background like unformed and indistinct lumps. The great outline of the church rose above this space with imposing solemnity, and the reddish light that shone in the top of its tower, where the guard maintained watch, imparted to this scene its final touch of chilling drama.

Even the air itself seemed to feed into that distressing situation. The night fell rapidly over the nearby hills, and as the wind passed through the deserted streets it produced that prolonged sad whistle it has at times, and which seemed like some mysterious voice of sobs and moaning. And to heighten the general fear of the residents, from time to time were heard the cries of the soldiers:

"Sentry . . . alert!" cried a stentorian voice from the town.

"Sentry . . . alert!" answered the other immediately from the roof of the jefe político's office.

"Sentry . . . alert!" repeated the third from the roof of the jail.

I do not know what it was in those sounds, coming as they did amid the shadows and silence, that set my nerves on edge. Some had a hoarse and strange quality; others were clear, even magnified, like some voice from the supernatural.

And so the night passed in this way, amid an atmosphere of general panic the influence of which must surely have caused the women to tremble and children to cry. When the light of dawn at last appeared, it eased our spirits; one by one the doors and windows opened, while people gradually walked once more in the streets and plazas. From their homes the residents asked one another what news they had heard, and alarming reports circulated, all borne of the troubled imaginations of cowed spirits. In reality no one knew anything.

At 6:00 in the morning, the bell in the tower sounded a call to arms. In an instant the public spaces emptied once more, and I heard nothing for a long time, other than the harsh slamming of doors and windows, all closing loudly and in haste. Soldiers once more occupied their vantage points, and some residents scurried to the tops of their houses, armed with pistols and rifles. Gun barrels glistened with dazzling brilliance in the top of the tower and in the windows of homes, illuminated by the rising sun, while potential combatants, their faces mostly agitated and trembling, prepared for battle. This anxious waiting went on for half an hour, until at last the jefe político came down from the bell tower where he had stationed himself with a telescope in order to survey the surrounding area and declared that there was nothing to fear. The pronunciados had indeed returned to cross through the edge of town, but having seen the inhabitants' activities, the riders took the long way around and were now far from Tequila. This news restored confidence in the hearts of the residents, and normal life soon resumed.

At noon I observed a new movement in the streets. One of my cousins went to the plaza to find out what was happening and then came back to explain what the hubbub was about.

"A servant has just come from La Florida with some news," he told me.

Keenly interested, I asked him, "What happened?"

"The pronunciados have committed some authentic savageries at that hacienda. They've ransacked the houses and then set them on fire, along with the granaries and the crops that were ready to be harvested. They've killed all the estate's animals that they found along the way, either shooting them or hacking them with machetes. And they haven't left so much as the most wretched hovel standing. When they finally headed out of La Florida, nothing remained but a mound of rubble."

"But have they harmed any of the people there?" I asked anxiously.

"Only one," answered my cousin. "The body of that one-eyed Analco has been found, lying outside his hut at the hacienda gate, with a bullet in his head. I don't know how it happened, and I don't know who killed him."

"And Don Santos?" I asked.

"The servant reports that with the pronunciados looking for him high and low, he barely had time to hide. He leapt into a precipice behind the hacienda. The fall injured his head and broke one of his legs, but despite it all he's alive."

"The Lord be praised!" I exclaimed, breathing deeply with relief. "He was lucky: if he'd fallen into their hands, all his money wouldn't have helped him."

"I believe it," replied my cousin. "They'd have squeezed him for all he was worth."

"They would have killed him," I tersely replied.

X.

A few days later I returned to Guadalajara. Because the *camino real*[69] passed within eyeshot, I was able to determine for myself the truth of the servant's account. The hacienda's main house, the barns, the straw huts: all had been reduced to a pile of rubble. The chapel that had been blessed less than a month earlier now looked like a building ravaged by time. Its exterior revealed the damage of the flames that had issued from the door and windows as tongues of fire had licked the sides. The hut where Nieves had lived now consisted of nothing more than ashes and a few calcified stones. No one remained at La Florida. Desolation had taken hold of these once happy and prosperous scenes. Thus pass the glories of this world.

Terrified by these events and even more by the awareness that Juan took part in the rebels' campaigns, Don Santos, scarcely healed from the fracture and the head wound he had endured, sold the hacienda, relocated to Guadalajara, and gave up on rural life altogether. To explain his decision, he asserted that in this nation it was impossible to live in the countryside, since the government provided no guarantees to hard-working people. What he should have said is that the authorities cannot free scoundrels like Don Santos from the consequences of their own misdeeds. But he does not confess this, and no one understands better than I the misleading nature of his remarks.

I have heard nothing more about Nieves. I fear that she has come to a bad end, because the hazardous life she took up upon leaving town can only make one suspect as much.

I haven't heard anything about Juan, either. By now he's probably a general.

The Bracelet

I.

I remember the scene as clearly and vividly as if I were living it right now, despite all the long years separating me from that moment.

It was near sunset on a day in May. The heat was suffocating; one could feel the heavy atmosphere like some warm liquid. At such hours Veracruz seemed an extension of Purgatory, and I was surprised to see that the houses, the ground, and even the bodies of the people did not burst into columns of smoke, like pieces of a world on fire. We found ourselves in a dark, silent furnace, without the burning red color or the sparks and crackles of the embers, but it was hot and painful, like San Lorenzo's grill of martyrdom.[1]

At the same time, though, the port offered a magnificent panorama. The setting sun was splendid as it reflected over the tranquil waters barely visible for the gentle warm breeze. In its limitless extension the immense mirror of the sea reproduced all the colors, tones, and hues of the sky, the atmosphere's diffuse light, and the images of the clouds whose long horizontal streaks of white matte lined the scene like parallel lines of snow. It was a festival of light and colors that danced on the water's burnished surface: a mixture of blue, gold, scarlet, pink, and amber, all melted into a visual reflection of joyful clarity.

Rita and I stood on the balcony of the hotel, our elbows on the railing, while her elderly aunt knitted in her room. We stood admiring the scene and enjoying the fresh air. Overcome by the painful stupor brought on by the idea of our approaching separation, we did nothing more than sigh quietly and gaze tenderly at one another.

In the distance glowered the gray-yellow mass of the fortress San

Juan de Ulúa,[2] like some sterile and insignificant rock, and close to its fortified protection, rocking gently and anchored at the foot of the island, floated the steamship that was to sail the next morning, carrying away from me the woman I so adored. It enraged me, like the presence of some hated enemy, and I wished that I could not see it, but wherever my eyes wandered, they always returned to that same sight.

Upon returning to Mexico after a prolonged absence, I had become the travel companion of an enchanting Cuban woman on the trip from Havana to Veracruz. With her elderly relative beside her she had come to the capital city of the Republic to fulfill her pious obligation to visit the tomb of a much-loved relative who lay at rest in Mexican soil.

After disembarking in La Heróica,[3] we continued on together to Mexico City, where I lost sight of her for a few days, during which period she dedicated herself to fulfilling the melancholy object of her journey. When I saw them once more, they were, as they say, with one foot on the gangplank to return to Havana. And I, following them as if their shadow, abandoned my own itinerary and returned with them on the train to Veracruz.[4] I lodged in the same hotel in order to maximize my time in the sweet company of Rita, even as I was about to lose her. I did so even if it was cruel of me to linger here, for my dear mother's broken health urgently demanded my presence in the faraway city where my family lived.[5]

It was during that time that my heart was filled with a deep tenderness toward this lovely foreigner. This object of my affection was more Gypsy than Spaniard. She was dark, and of that fiery complexion that makes one think she lived with emotions constantly raised and senses always tensed. That impression owed in part to the blackness of her large, flashing eyes and her long lashes, to the lustrous ebony of her skin, and to the pronounced crimson of the full lips that moved so gracefully over her fine, tightly set teeth. The rest of her body and person formed a symmetry with these features: the smoothness of her waist, the gracefulness of her movements, the soft delicacy of her hands, and the impassioned timbre of her accent and her laugh.

But in contrast to these placid charms, Rita's bearing and actions suggested a certain hint of sadness, some undefined shadow that lent chiaroscuro to her beauty. She always wore black or dark-colored clothes, concealed her face behind thick veils, and evaded the ways and company of others, always setting herself apart from lively crowds and avoiding conversation. So stark a contradiction between the person and her conduct had awakened in my soul an ever-deepening interest in this young woman, because by nature I am drawn toward things shrouded and mysterious.

My courtesy toward Rita and her aunt during the sea voyage and my insistence on accompanying them everywhere, even when they objected, and in those moments when they showed a certain coolness toward me: little by little these attentions wore away the enchanting Cuban's resistance, until once we were in Mexico City, I had the satisfaction of seeing my affection returned.

Very shortly afterward we put our plans in order. Rita would return to Havana, and I would separate from her just long enough to see to my mother and to briefly look over those matters that had gone unattended in my absence. Once my mother recovered her health and my affairs were in order, I would head for Cuba, where we would formalize our union.

II.

Even though our separation was to be brief, however, we were both quite downcast that afternoon.

"Tomorrow at this time," I told her, "you will be far, far away from me."

"Yes," she replied, "and very sad, because I won't see you."

"Not as sad as I, for you're taking all the joy out of my heart and all the light from my eyes."

"Really?" she continued in a child-like tone. "Will you miss me terribly?"

"Terribly," I replied, almost inaudibly.

"I will do nothing but cry until I see your smile once more."

"Look," I told her, "there's the ship that's going to take you far away from me. I hate it."

"That accursed thing. To me it looks like a monster that's going to carry me to some terrible end."

The shadows continued to fall little by little. The atmosphere's brilliance dimmed, and the waves of the gulf gently began to peak, tinting the distance with a vague whiteness. Close up they appeared a steely gray, almost lead, and their color grew deeper by the moment. The air seemed everywhere infused with the melancholy of the "Hail, Mary," a farewell to light, to life, to happiness, and a plaintive sigh of protest and despair rose against the threshold of the night. The spirit of sadness enveloped us all around, turning the world pale, hurling ideas of sadness in our very faces, and weighing down our hearts with an unspeakable anxiety.

Rita and I stood silent for a few moments, submersed in the sea of melancholy that surrounded us. But our eyes still conversed.

"Rita," I at last murmured, taking hold of her right hand, "promise me to be true, and to love me as much as I long for you."

"Faithful even to death," she replied, taking my hand in nervous emotion.

"Now that you're leaving," I continued, "I would like you to leave me something of yours that I can take with me, and that will ease my bitterness, a sweet gift that will give me strength by its memory of you, something that I can always have before me, as if it were your portrait."

"I've already given you flowers, locks of my hair, rings, relics, portraits. . . ."

"That's true," I said, "but they aren't enough."

"What else do you want, Enrique? Tell me, and I'll give it to you."

I remained silent for a moment as I meditated over my choice. There was nothing else to ask of her, for I already had all of those things that one solicits and receives from a lover. But as I held her hand the tips of my fingers touched the hard surface of her bracelet, that bracelet that she never removed from her wrist. Suddenly my mind was made up. Wide, thick, and heavy, that particular piece of jewelry had the look of a handcuff that binds a prisoner's arm: the same massiveness, the same crude exterior. Only the value of the metal and the shine of its surface broke the resemblance, perfect in all other regards. The most unusual thing was that the Cuban wore it always, both day and night, whether during a visit or when taking a stroll, adapting it to all clothing and circumstances. On one occasion I had asked Rita why she was so fond of the bracelet, and she answered, not a little embarrassed, that it was a family heirloom.

Such antecedents and details were in fact the light that drew me to the bracelet. Of course, Rita valued it so highly that she never went anywhere without it. It was steeped in her person. And it was therefore ideal for my purposes.

"The bracelet," I said forcefully. "Give me the bracelet."

"The bracelet!" she responded with agitation.

"Yes. Give it to me."

"Why do you want it?"

"Because you're never without it. Because it goes with you everywhere."

"No, not that. Something else. . . ."

"No. It has to be that."

"Why the insistence? I can give you something better."

"There is nothing better."

"I'll give you my hair. You've often praised its abundance and dark color. Cut off a lock with your own hand and keep it. It's a part of me."

"No, Rita, it has to be as I said."

"Impossible, Enrique."

"Why? We're going to see," I said with emotion. "Why is it impossible?"

She hesitated for a moment, and as I held her hand, I could feel it trembling.

"It's unfortunate," she went on, "that you should have this idea. Why did it occur to you?"

"It's nothing more than happenstance," I replied as vague instinctive jealousies began to prick at me. "Now I'm coming to know you. All the worse if you're false and deceiving."

"Don't insult me. Have I given you motive to do so?"

"You're tearing my soul apart with suspicion."

"How unhappy I am! And unable to please you!"

"Even if I'm dying of jealousy?"

Rita could only sob in response.

"Even if I were to believe that you don't love me?" I persisted.

"That you are a betrayer and faithless, and that the love you have sworn for me was nothing more than a joke?"

"I love you with all my heart, as God is my witness."

"If that's true, then give me the bracelet."

"I can't, Enrique."

"Why not?"

"No."

"If that's the case," I continued angrily, "why deceive me? You're keeping secrets from me. I don't know who you are, or what your past is. . . ."

"Enrique! Enrique!"

"And I need to know you. . . ."

"Do not doubt my love; I ask you on bended knee!"

"I doubt . . . yes. That's all that's lacking: that I not doubt you."

"Don't you know that you are torturing me?"

"And don't you see that you are killing me?"

It was a long, painful scene filled with recriminations and sarcasm, with threats and demands, until at last Rita began to cry out loud. But instead of inspiring tenderness, her tears only irritated me further.

"For the last time," I shouted, my temper roused by the argument, "will you give me the bracelet? Yes or no?"

"I repeat that I cannot."

"Then goodbye. I'm leaving."

"No, don't go," she said passionately as she seized my arm.

"The bracelet!"

"Have pity. . . ."

"It's useless . . . the bracelet! The bracelet!'

And when no answer came, I tore my arm from her hands forcefully, and filled with rage I stormed off, a man blinded by fury.

III.

It was a feverish night. In a single moment the world had changed for me, and my fortune had suffered a terrible shock. That which I had held most certain, that which had mattered most to me, that which had sunk its deepest roots in the heart: it had slipped through my hands, abandoned me, disappeared altogether. Rita was suddenly absent from my life; she had fled from my arms, evaporated from my lips like water, and instead of her grace and tenderness, and instead of the promised happiness, all that remained was a deep, dark pit in my soul.

I spent mournful hours turning in my bed as if on a rack, my brain on fire, my heart calling me to arms with blood raging through its narrow veins and beating in my temples like a hammer. What was the meaning of this mystery? Why had Rita offered anything rather than part with the bracelet? Who had given it to her? To whom had she been faithful and submissive? The bracelet surely did not come from her parents, nor from some friend or relative, for if so she would have had no shame telling me so. She had remained silent, and her silence was as transparent as glass: it announced, and loudly, that it was a token of love. A love token, and yet she said that she cared for me! A love token, and yet she wanted to be my wife! The woman had no scruples; she was a monster. Then who was she, really? Perhaps an adventuress?

My whole being shook with rage and sorrow as I asked myself these questions. It seemed to me impossible that there were people as depraved as her, and I cursed the hour when we had met.

But as I struggled with these ideas, a passion rose in my heart, a passion that was glowing and tragic but also firm and invincible, like a rock battered by water. The same mystery that enveloped this young woman, and even the dishonorable conduct that her behavior suggested, had fed in my heart the same tragic fascination one feels toward some drama or abyss. I could not conceive of permanently separating from her, nor could I force myself to part from her forever. It seemed as if the world had become a desert, that the sun was dying in the heavens, that all the flowers in the world had dried up, that all the stars would be extinguished, and all music silenced, and that my heart would freeze and stop beating within my head, like the pendulum of some broken clock.

Throughout this anguished crisis, the bracelet persistently flashed in my imagination. It seemed to me to be made of flames, of red-hot embers, of brass repoussé. I could see it: wide, thick, strong, its two ends joined together by a tiny but inviolable lock; and I guessed that it was impossible to open, and that it clung to its owner's flesh with invisible force. That vision tortured me. It was in vain that I tried to banish it from my fantasies; the rebellious image returned time and again as my brain ran in circles like a firefly flitting in the darkness.

I spent the night in this fashion, the prisoner of my own anguish. As the first rays of sunlight filtered through the railing of the balcony, they found me with my eyes open, broken and feverish. The servants had already awakened, and whispers of life were running through the city when exhaustion at last overcame me, and I slept. My slumbers were poor and agitated; the same contention of ideas and visions continued in my brain, the same that had tormented me throughout the night. But now all was more leaden and confused than before, as if my spirit had been enchained and was to be handed over to martyrdom.

It was broad daylight when I awoke. Upon beholding the sun, I immediately felt that sense of security that comes from escaping from some horrible nightmare. But my consciousness of the situation returned, and I found reality even worse than my terrifying dreams.

I quickly rose, shattered in both body and soul, and went to the hallway to see what was happening with Rita. A servant was waiting for me before the door of my room. Upon seeing me he handed over a letter. It was from her. With my heart pounding and trembling with emotion, I opened the envelope and read. It said:

"My adored Enrique:

"I'm writing these lines as I prepare to board. I need to see you to give you an explanation. I've spent a frightful night. If you don't want me to die, don't deny me this favor. Yours forever, Rita."

IV.

The morning was radiant. No cloud darkened the clear blue sky, no light mist gauzed the air. The sun had begun to climb toward its zenith. It filled the day with dazzling clarity and crowned the waves with vivid gold. The afternoon heat had yet to descend upon us. The port was filled with hectic activity as vessels prepared to embark. Wherever one went in the bay, one saw small crafts loaded with passengers and freight, or else returning empty and in search of new cargo, all leaving the harbor for the ships. This panorama, so smiling and full of life, lay before my eyes as I rowed toward the steamship where Rita awaited me, but it failed to calm the anxiety in my heart. The letter I had received gave me hope, but I felt an instinctive alarm when I thought of the promised explanation. A presentiment told me that it was something serious, and I feared what her revelation might be.

Once I leapt on board, I saw no one but Rita, as if she were alone in that place. She too had come here without concern for anyone else, and by tacit agreement we sought refuge in the most remote place possible.

She was dressed in white. Her long, black hair curled down her back, and wide sleeves only half-concealed those bare and shapely arms of incomparable perfection. Insomnia had dimmed somewhat the color of her cheeks and traced dark circles under her large eyes. Broken, melancholy, sorrowful, she looked to me more beautiful and enchanting than ever. I contemplated her with delirious eyes, enfolding her in looks of passion, while she stared at me straight on with eyes wide open and fixed on mine, as if she understood my desire to take in her loveliness and wished to come flying to answer my call.

And we both trembled with identical convulsions, as if shaken by the same electrical current. She told me, "I haven't the strength to leave without seeing you once more. Any other woman would have given up after last night's scene. But not I, because I love you to the point of adoration, and with all of my soul."

As she spoke these words, she desperately grasped my right hand with her own and held it tightly over her heart. I could feel the power of it beating. An immense tenderness overcame me, and I immediately forgot about everything else, but there on her bare arm I saw the bracelet, and my anger returned.

"I'm going to explain everything," she went on, intuiting what I was thinking. "No one knows this secret other than you . . . and God in heaven. It is a terrible confession that costs me painful effort, but you deserve to know everything. I want you to know everything, even if I should die, even if it kills me. You own my life and my fortune, and I place everything in your hands."

I felt myself turning a ghastly pale on hearing her speak this way, for I foresaw the immensity of the revelation, and after turning wildly like some frightened bird, my heart settled, weak and humble. Rita's face also turned pale, and I felt her hand twist as I held it.

"I was only a girl," she said. "I was barely fifteen years old when I came to Mexico for the first time. I traveled with my parents, who of course were still alive at that time, the occasion being an invitation to the wedding of my mother's sister. My aunt was a woman over forty years old, almost an old lady, and we were very much surprised by her plans to marry. But we were even more surprised when we met Teodoro, her fiancé, a man ten years younger than her, handsome and gentlemanly.

"Once the ceremony had concluded, my family and I remained in the newlyweds' home for a short time. After all, it made no sense to return abruptly following so long a trip.[6]

"I ought not and do not want to enter into details, for they would torment both you and myself. Teodoro and I were young and saw one another constantly. A sympathetic attraction formed between us. . . . I don't know how, but we grew close together, little by little, unconsciously, until that moment least expected, when we found ourselves in love and confessed that love to each other.

"Wait, Enrique, don't rush to judge, and don't be blind. That expression on your face frightens me. Hear me out.

"I can scarcely describe the difficulties and the anguish of our situation. Even though my inexperience did not allow me to understand fully the horrors in which we found ourselves, I had a vague, instinctual awareness of them. I felt guilty, but there was a stabbing pleasure in my anguish, and I walked about blindly, neither knowing what would become of me nor how our mad love would end. We had no hopes, nor could we confess to the world that we loved each other. We had to treat each other with feigned indifference, and it's not to tell the pain and alarm caused by that life of deceit and hypocrisy. But in spite of everything we never lost our discretion, and no one, not even my sainted mother, who watched over me so painstakingly, nor my beloved aunt, who was by nature jealous and untrusting, ever came to suspect that there was something between us.

"It was thanks to my lucky star that, despite everything, Teodoro's soul was not depraved. And for that reason I was spared from shame and dishonor. My tender age and ignorance of the world in which I had been raised had left me weak and helpless in the face of that horrible crisis. But no impure thoughts entered my spirit; I was satisfied by Platonic love, however forbidden, and I would have deserved nothing more for the future than to live forever a prisoner in that profound martyrdom.

"But the same did not hold true for Teodoro, as I was later to realize. He appeared depressed, angry, and often tore himself away from me when we were close, saying, 'I love you so much that you are sacred to me. I will never give you cause for complaint. I would rather die . . . die a thousand times over.' But I did not understand the true meaning of his words.

"The situation was growing more difficult by the day, and Teodoro fell into such an emotional state that I was frightened. He cursed his luck and his marriage and cried like a child when he reflected on the impossibility of our happiness.

"One day, in the worst moment of the crisis, my father announced his decision that we return to Havana. This brought on a fever that made Teodoro almost delirious. I also felt stricken out of my mind. But my condition was nothing compared to the extreme to which he fell.

"The night before our departure from Mexico, we found ourselves alone for a few moments.

"'You're laughing,' he told me, his face tormented, 'and I cannot follow you. When will we see each other again? I have no right to expect anything from you, but as a supreme favor, as a concession toward one who is dying, promise me that you will agree to one thing.' With tears in my eyes, I promised that I would; and at that moment he took out this same bracelet, which he had been hiding in his pocket.

"'Accept this to remember me,' he said, 'Allow me to place it on your wrist. It has a lock. I want to turn the key with my own hand. Now, promise me that you will never take it off until I open it for you, and that during that time—and only during that time—you will never belong to another man.'

"And I promised him the same, and from the bottom of my heart.

"'Thank you,' he murmured, glowing with delight. 'May heaven reward you for the infinite kindness you show me.' And torn with emotion, he kissed my hand and went away sobbing.

"That same night, shortly before dawn, the household awoke to the sound of an explosion. After a quick search we came upon Teodoro in his room. He lay at the foot of a great mirror, a revolver in his hand, and his head blown open by a bullet.

"Five years have passed since that moment, and yet I still see him. And so, Enrique," Rita concluded, trembling and sobbing, "this is the explanation I owed you. Now kill me if you wish but know that I love you more than my own life."

"And the other?" I roared furiously.

"It was confusion, youth, inexperience. Any fifteen-year-old girl can be victim of a mistake like that. Have pity on me. Don't condemn me."

"If that's the case, give me the bracelet."

The young woman hesitated for a moment. Meanwhile, the hour of departure had come. I heard the anchors being hoisted and in my confusion saw the urgency of the sailors' efforts as they prepared to embark. The crying and rapture of the moment heightened my emotions.

"The bracelet!" I shouted with a harsh voice.

"I cannot," Rita murmured with a dejected look.

"Then you still love your accomplice?" I asked, half-crazed.

"No," the young woman replied, raising her head.

"In that case give it to me and let's put an end to the matter. We've no time to lose."

Rita began to cry and answered with a broken voice:

"I don't want to be ungrateful to someone who loved me, and who gave his life for me . . . I don't want to . . . I shouldn't . . . I can't."

Her refusal somehow calmed my frenzied state. And then came a repugnant scene that I can only recall with confusion. I seized Rita's hand and with my own taut, nervous fingers tried to tear away the bracelet.

"You must be mine," I said, "and this bracelet has come between us. But I'll take it from you even if you resist. I'll take it by force."

She did not try to resist; rather, she gave me her arm, and I squeezed it, shook it, bruised it, all without pity and without consideration. The families and friends of those about to depart were now descending the ladder, and the steamship's whistle signaled that the moment had come.

And I, without stopping to think of anything else, and without bothering to conceal what I was doing, kept up my fruitless struggle to seize that hateful piece of jewelry. But it clung tightly around her arm and allowed no space for my hand. My brutality was all in vain.

At last, after a few moments of this sterile attack, she murmured sadly: "Enrique, you're hurting me. I cannot remove the bracelet. Do you not see that it has a lock?"

"Then give me the key. Give it to me!"

"I don't have it."

"Lies!"

"I do not lie: he carried it with him to the grave."

The effect of these words on me was indescribable: *"He carried it with him to the grave!"* They struck me like some evil omen. Cold terror circulated through my veins, and at that moment I saw before me the grave, the dead man, the crime. An ocean of horror came between the woman and me. It seemed that Rita could belong to no other man but the suicide, that she was prisoner within that same tomb, and that the bracelet was the symbol of her perpetual captivity.

And without knowing what I was doing, I let go of her arm and went to the boat's exit, fled down the stairs, and leapt into the skiff that was waiting to carry me to the port.

The time was upon us. Balancing over the waves the boat now began its departure.

A voice caused me to turn and look upward. It was Rita's voice. Leaning against the rail, her face covered in tears, she called my name.

"Enrique! Enrique! Goodbye, my love!"

And placing both hands to her lips, she blew me repeated and tender kisses.

And I, ecstatic, confused, unconscious of myself, watched her move away, my eyes now cold, watching as one watches youth, the years, even life itself slip away and disappear over the horizon, taking with them everything that is dear to us on earth.

Notes

INTRODUCTION

1. *Obras de Lic. D. J. López Portillo y Rojas* (Mexico City: V. Agüero, 1898–1909), 4 vols. This is available through a variety of online sources, including Google Books and Biblioteca Virtual Miguel de Cervantes. "El boleto de lotería" comes from volume 3 (1903), 25–96. "El Espejo" is from volume 2 (1900), 303–42. *Nieves* can be found in volume 2 (1900), 7–137, while the final selection, "El brazalete," appears in volume 2 (1900), 345–72.

2. A *caudillo* was a regional leader whose authority derived not from institutional sources, such as constitutions or elections, but rather from economic power, family connections, and charismatic authority. The term derives from the medieval Spanish reconquest of the Iberian Peninsula; in that context, it might be translated as "warlord." Much of Mexico's postrevolutionary history involves the campaign to subordinate such figures to national authority.

3. Ángel Rama, *La ciudad letrada* (Hanover, NH: Ediciones del Norte, 1984), 38, 82–83, 111–27.

4. Ana G. Valenzuela-Zapata and Gary Paul Nabham, *¡Tequila! A Natural and Cultural History* (Tucson: University of Arizona Press, 2003), 7–11.

5. José María Muriá, "Momentos del tequila: El agave histórico," in *El Tequila: Arte tradicional de México*, ed. Alberto Ruy Sánchez Lacy and Margarita de Orellana (Mexico City: Artes de México, 2008), third edition, 20–21. See also "A History of the World's Oldest Tequila Brand" at the Cuervo website.

6. The reconstruction of the López Portillo's genealogy and la Rojeña estate history comes from a variety of sources. See Margarita de Orrellana, "Microhistoria del tequila: El caso Cuervo," in *El Tequila*, 16–25. For genealogical tracing I have relied on the extremely helpful information provided on the Geni website.

7. *Excélsior*, Feb. 17, 2014.

8. Josefina MacGregor, "José López Portillo y Rojas," in *Cancilleres de México: 1910–1988* (Mexico City: Secretaría de Relaciones Exteriores, 1992),

98–100. This extended entry, part of MacGregor's collected biographies of Mexico's secretaries of Foreign Relations, is actually one of our most comprehensive sources on López Portillo's life.

9. Valenzuela-Zapata and Nabham, 17.

10. MacGregor, 100.

11. Francois-Xavier Guerra, *México del antiguo régimen a la revolución*, trans. Sergio Fernández Bravo (Mexico City: Fondo de Cultura Económica, 2010), 60–64. The original edition appeared in 1985.

12. Roland Grass, *José López Portillo y Rojas: A Novelist of Social Reform in Mexico before the Revolution of 1910* (Macomb, IL: Western Illinois Press, 1970), 2.

13. MacGregor, 107.

14. MacGregor, 109–11.

15. José María Muriá, *Breve historia de Jalisco* (Guadalajara: Secretaría de Educación Pública, 1988), 459.

16. Henry Bamford Parkes, *A History of Mexico* (New York: Houghton Mifflin Company, 1969), 332. Originally published in 1938.

17. Summarized from chapter 4 of Robert Curley's *Citizens and Believers: Religion and Politics in Revolutionary Jalisco, 1900–1930* (Albuquerque: University of New Mexico Press, 2018).

18. MacGregor, 112, thinks that this essay was what landed López Portillo the job as secretary of Foreign Relations, but I suspect the appointment followed rather more complex motives, such as keeping a potential trouble-maker close at hand.

19. Rama, 127.

20. See José María Muriá, *Breve historia de Jalisco* (Guadalajara: Universidad de Jalisco, 1988), 377–82. Muriá actually credits López Portillo with founding *La República Literaria*, but sixteen seems a bit young for a literary kingpin, particularly one whose parents were about to send him out of the country.

21. Alberto Ruy Sánchez y Lacy and Margarita de Orellano, eds., *El tequila: Arte tradicional de México*, 3rd ed. (México: Artes de México, 2008). Originally published in 1995.

22. Edited by Salvador Botello, this handsome work is available in the University of Texas Libraries' Nettie Lee Benson Latin American Collection.

23. Doris Sommer, *Foundational Fictions: The National Romances of Latin America* (Berkeley: University of California Press, 1992), 225.

24. On this point I am indebted to the insights of Susan M. Rigdon's *The Culture Facade: Art, Science, and Politics in the Work of Oscar Lewis* (Urbana: University of Illinois Press, 1988), particularly 40–45.

25. See two instructive studies of the Lozada uprising: Michele McArdle Stephens, *In the Lands of Fire and Sun: Resistance and Accommodation in the*

Huichol Sierra, 1723–1930 (Lincoln: University of Nebraska Press, 2018), and Zachary Brittsan, *Popular Politics and Rebellion in Mexico: Manuel Lozada and La Reforma, 1855–1876* (Nashville: Vanderbilt University Press, 2015).

26. Brittsan, 6, 16, 26, 77.

27. José M. Vigil, "La Reforma," in *México a través de los siglos*, ed. Vicente Riva Palacio, vol. 9: 254, 325 (Mexico City: Editorial Cumbre, 1962). Originally published in 1884.

28. Brittsan, 37–47.

29. Stephens, 49–54.

30. Brittsan, 38–40, 138–45.

31. For an overview of the bandit theme (followed by careful case studies in subsequent chapters), see Juan Pablo Dabove, *Nightmares of the Lettered City: Banditry and Literature in Latin America, 1816–1929* (Pittsburgh: University of Pittsburgh Press, 2007), 1–12.

32. I explore the role of the jefe político in the Yucatecan context in *Rebellion Now and Forever: Mayas, Hispanics, and Caste War Violence, 1800–1880* (Stanford: Stanford University Press, 2009), 25–31, 308–12.

33. Friedrich Katz, *The Life and Times of Pancho Villa* (Stanford: Stanford University Press, 1998), 805.

34. I am indebted here to Juan José Reyes's instructive *Cuestión de suerte* (Mexico City: Clío, 1997), 40–55.

35. George M. Foster introduced this concept in what is certainly one of the most famous anthropology articles ever written: "Peasant Society and the Image of Limited Good," *American Anthropologist* 67 (2) (1965), 293–315.

36. Muriá, 337–42.

37. Muriá, 399–408.

38. Valenzuela-Zapata and Nabhan, 55–61.

39. Edgar Allen Poe, *The Complete Tales and Poems of Edgar Allen Poe*, introduction by Wilbur C. Scott (New York: Castle Books, 2002), 285–91. Originally published in 1985.

40. See Kathryn A. Sloan, *Runaway Daughters: Seduction, Elopement, and Honor in Nineteenth-Century Mexico* (Albuquerque: University of New Mexico Press, 2008), 33–35.

41. Sommer, 1–4.

42. Helen Delpar, *The Enormous Vogue of Things Mexican: Cultural Relations between the United States and Mexico, 1920–1935* (Tuscaloosa: University of Alabama Press, 1992); John S. Brushwood, *Mexico and Its Novel: A Nation's Search for Identity* (Austin: University of Texas Press, 1966), 119–22; Walter M. Langford, *The Mexican Novel Comes of Age* (Notre Dame: University of Notre Dame Press, 1971), 1–12. A somewhat fuller treatment and greater recogni-

tion feature in Carlos González Peña, *History of Mexican Literature*, trans. Gusta Barfield Nance and Florene Johnson Dunstan, 3rd. ed. (Dallas: Southern Methodist University Press, 1968), 317–18, originally published in 1943.

THE LOTTERY TICKET

1. The British author Samuel Smiles's *Self-Help* (1859) was a nineteenth-century bestseller. It argued for the role of individual initiative and persistence as guarantors of success. By 1900 it had been translated into many languages.

2. Guano (bird or bat droppings) constituted a major source of commercial fertilizer before the creation of synthetic substitutes. Much of it was mined on the coasts of Latin America.

3. In Latin America (and in many other societies), to beg for alms at the doors of the church was one of the lowest positions to which a person could fall. The image is more than a mere figure of speech.

4. Mesoamerica only has two seasons: a dry season, running from November to May, and a rainy season extending from June to October. The dependable alternation of these two periods has formed the basis of agriculture from time beyond memory, even though global warming has rejiggered somewhat the meteorological dependability of old.

5. *Zarzuela* was a form of music-hall production popular in both Spain and Latin America. Excelling in dance numbers and catchy melodies, it aimed at middle to lower classes.

6. As discussed in this volume's introduction, the theme of positivist philosophy informs much of López Portillo y Rojas's life and work. In this case, he pokes fun at the stark materialism that informs this philosophy.

7. A *zarabanda*, or sarabande, is a type of Spanish dance, set in triple meter, that dates back to the Muslim occupation (711–1492). Over time, it became a popular folk dance in much of Latin America.

8. The term *seven sleepers* refers to a legend of seven Christian soldiers from the city of Ephesus, today an archaeological site on the west coast of Turkey. Faced with performing forced pagan ceremonies under the cruel Roman emperor Decius (reign 249–51), the soldiers sealed themselves in a cave and fell into a miraculous sleep. They supposedly awoke when the cave was opened three centuries later. The seven sleepers recounted their story to the amazement of all, then promptly died.

9. That is, Damiana herself.

10. The monetary system of pesos and centavos (1:100) replaced the ancient Spanish coinage of *reales*, *medios*, and *cuartos* in the 1860s, but the terms *peso* and *real* were used interchangeably for quite some time thereafter.

11. Iztaccíhuatl, Nahuatl for "white woman," together with its fellow vol-

cano Popocatépetl, lies along the border between the states of Mexico and Puebla. At 5,320 feet, it enjoys a permanent snowcap that suggested the profile of a woman lying face-up. Significantly more visible in López Portillo's pollution-free times, these two volcanos formed a central part of the Valley of Mexico's visual landscape.

12. This list of impossible tasks was a way of accusing Blas of being a dreamer. The so-called Aztec calendar is in fact a monument to the Mexica sun god Tonatiuh. It was unearthed in 1790 during remodeling of the Mexico City cathedral. Emblematic not only of Mexica culture but of Mexico itself, it today stands in a prominent location in the great Museo de Antropología.

13. Presumably a reference to the gold domes of St. Basil's Cathedral in the Kremlin, constructed in the 1500s under the legendarily unstable Ivan the Terrible.

14. José Antonio López de Santa Anna (1794–1876), a Veracruz-born general, dominated much of Mexican national life in the first half century following independence in 1821.

15. The specific euphemism that Conchita uses is "*noticias de Francia*," or "news from France."

16. The Avenida de la Reforma, personally designed by ersatz Emperor Maximilian and modeled on the Champs Élysées in Paris, begins at Mexico City's Parque Alameda and runs to Bosques de Chapultepec, 5.4 kilometers to the southwest. Carriage rides and strolls through the Paseo and the Bosques were obligatory for upper-crust Porfirians, a practice that Diego Rivera mercilessly lampooned in his murals.

The Mirror

1. The word *luna* normally means "the moon," but in somewhat older Spanish also referred to the round mirror found on top of women's dressers. López Portillo uses the term as a furniture reference in the story's penultimate section, suggesting that its appearance here is an intentional ambiguity.

2. Bartolomé Esteban Murillo (1617–1682) was one of Spain's finest baroque painters. He specialized in Counter-Reformation religious themes, particularly the Immaculate Conception. Murillo died in Cádiz as a result of falling from a scaffolding while painting a mural of the marriage of St. Catherine.

3. An *alumbrado* (or, in the case of women, *alumbrada*) is a Catholic term for someone who claims mystical access to divine will unmediated by either ecclesiastical or biblical authority. The idea here is that Aurora spoke like an impassioned mystic.

4. "*Ah barro miserable, eternamente / No podrás ni aun sufrir!*" These lines come from "Rima LIXV," by Spanish romantic poet Gustavo Adolfo Bécquer

(1836–1870). In this poem Bécquer bemoans the fact that not even his grief is permanent.

5. A *tertulia* was a form of social gathering common among well-to-do Latin American families in the nineteenth century. It could take many forms but often involved music, conversations, and refreshments in parlors or gardens.

6. "The Mirror" has no obvious setting, but this simple detail grounds it in Porfirian Mexico. Part of the mid-century Liberal reform involved secularizing ceremonies of life passage such as birth, marriage, and death. And while most Mexicans continued to see a church wedding as the real wedding, it was first necessary to obtain a marriage certificate at the *registro civil* (civil registry). Then as now most couples treat this step as a nothing more than a wedding license.

7. Here López Portillo uses the term *luna* to refer to the mirror itself. Originally a reference to the mounted, round mirrors above a woman's dresser (as used here), it later became synonymous with any round mirror and loosely became another term for a mirror of any sort.

Nieves

1. As explained in the introduction, *Nieves* draws heavily from the legends surrounding Manuel Lozada. His uprising and his final defeat in 1873 form a historical watershed for Jalisco history.

2. Then as now, the "Hail, Mary," or "Angelus" prayer, was often associated with moments of desperation.

3. Alaric was the Visigoth king who led the sack of Rome in 410. Genseric, or Gaeseric, led the Vandals to perform the same destructive act forty-six years later.

4. "Little nipple."

5. López Portillo uses the term "mezcal" interchangeably to refer to both the agave plant and the liquor produced from it. This translation aims for a more discriminating approach.

6. The Reform War (1858–60) was a defining event of nineteenth-century Mexico. Conservative adherents to the colonial way of life rebelled against a Liberal government intent on fostering capitalism, individual initiative, juridical equality, and separation of church and state. The Liberal Party under President Benito Juárez ultimately prevailed, but only after the country suffered appalling bloodshed and destruction. Defeated Conservatives repaired to Europe, where they promoted an intervention on the part of the French government. The Liberals prevailed in this struggle as well, and the tottering interventionist government was definitively ousted in 1867.

7. A slightly misleading word choice on the part of López Portillo. The

"seeds" are rather runners sent up from a dying plant. These are known as *hijos*, or "sons."

8. A *cura* is the priest charged with managing a parish. Then as now, curas were expected to minister to the faithful throughout their often far-flung territory. Given their higher degree of education, their links to a larger organization, and above all the prestige of their person, curas occupied an enormously important role in rural Mexico during the colonial and early national periods.

9. The *mano* and *metate* are the paired stone tools used, from time beyond memory, for grinding soaked corn kernels into dough. A *comal* is a large, flat griddle used mainly for cooking tortillas.

10. A *rebozo* is a scarf, measuring approximately 28 by 70 inches (0.71 by 1.77 meters) and with a fringe at each end. It can be made of silk, cotton, or wool. Versatile in use, the rebozo has long been an essential article in the wardrobes of Mexican women.

11. Probably a reference to malaria, which was endemic throughout much of rural Mexico and the circum-Caribbean. Malaria ranks alongside smallpox as one of the great killers in human history.

12. *Hoja de gigante (Anthurium ellipticum)*, also known as Jungle King. The plant is indigenous to Mexico but now occupies a prominent place in gardening throughout the world.

13. The term *amo* was a common and highly deferential way of referring to the property owner. Today it is most commonly used to refer to the owner of a pet.

14. In the days before industrially processed and mass-marketed tobacco, corn-husk cigars and cigarettes were common throughout rural Mexico.

15. *Vuestra Merced*, or "Your Mercy," was a common term of deference in the colonial and nineteenth-century periods. Though it has largely disappeared from modern Mexican parlance, it can still be heard in other regions of Latin America.

16. The word *frastero* is a corruption of *forastero*, a rather antiquated term for an outsider. As such, it amounts to a slang version of an archaism.

17. The term *en mala amistad* literally means "in bad friendship." A more idiomatic translation might be "lives in sin," but I have left it in to retain the quaintness of the original Spanish.

18. In other words, "Don't be a hick."

19. The term *tapextle* refers any item of rustic furniture made from tough, dried vines or sticks. It variously served as a bed, a trunk, or a chair, among other uses.

20. As gazelles do not have blue eyes, that earlier reference probably indicates that Nieves's eyes were large and round.

21. The term *campesino* is elastic. In its most limited sense, it simply refers to anyone who makes a living in the countryside. But its actual usage usually signals poverty and disenfranchisement.

22. It is unclear whether López Portillo refers to the national capital of Mexico City or the state capital of Guadalajara. He would have been personally familiar with both, but given the novel's western setting, Guadalajara seems the more likely of the two.

23. La Barranca del Río Santiago, which López Portillo describes in loving detail in this chapter, has been renowned for its natural beauty. In 2024 the federal government declared it a protected zone.

24. Although the depths of the canyon undoubtedly lacked a breeze, they were by no means short on oxygen, given the hyperabundant plant life.

25. The *trapiche* was a fixture of rural Latin America and the Caribbean. Derived from Arabic technology, it consists of vertically arranged grinding cylinders, turned by wind, water, or animal power, and used to crush sugar cane.

26. In Greek mythology the Garden of Hesperides belonged to Hera, queen of the gods, and was located somewhere beyond the western Atlas Mountain range of modern-day Morocco. It provided a home and playground for the nymphs but was famous for its grove of apple trees that produced the solid gold fruit that figures prominently in that same mythology. Eris, goddess of strife, stole one such apple and threw it into the midst of a banquet to which she had not been invited. The apple bore the legend "To the most beautiful goddess." This "gift" naturally caused a fierce competition among the other goddesses, who settled on Paris of Troy to arbitrate. Aphrodite, goddess of love, successfully bribed Paris by promising him Helen, who just so happened to be married to Menelaus, King of Sparta. The rest, as they say, is history.

27. The mamey tree *(Mamea americana)* is native to Mesoamerica and the Caribbean. Both mamey and mango trees reach enormous heights in rain-rich southeast Mexico, but the sight of these Yucatecan and Tabascan "colossi" would possibly have been unfamiliar to López Portillo. Mango trees *(Mandifera indica)* came from India, southeast Asia, and the Philippines, but by the late nineteenth century they had spread throughout Mesoamerica.

28. Ignacio Altamirano (1834–1893) was a celebrated man of letters. He was born in Guerrero of Chontal extraction and went on to participate in the Liberal reform. He is best known for the posthumously published *El Zarco* (1901), often considered the height of Porfirian novels, even though Manuel Sánchez Mármol's *Antón Pérez* (1903) is arguably superior in most regards.

29. An odd comment on the part of the narrator's cousin, since regional pride usually demanded that the women thereof surpassed all others in appearance, regardless of where in Mexico one happened to be.

30. The gusla, or gusle, is a one-string bowed musical instrument that is used often to accompany the epic folk balladeers of southeast Europe. Neapolitan painters used it to conjure up images of a romanticized peasantry.

31. The original *matrimoneoado*, in all its atrocious splendor, is yet another of López Portillo's occasional attempts to capture unlettered rural dialect.

32. Amatitán is a small town eleven kilometers southeast of Tequila on the road to Guadalajara.

33. "Cross-eyed blonde." The ugly duckling turned swan was a trusty device of Porfirian novels; see, for example, the story of Rosalba in *Antón Pérez*, by Miguel Sánchez Mármol.

34. *Jefes políticos* were linchpins of Porfirian administration. A legacy of the late colonial period, the jefe was a district-level, gubernatorially appointed figure whose main job, we might say, was "to keep an eye on things," not only in terms of lower-class unrest, but also of corrupt, politically ambitious, and even criminally inclined creoles and mestizos (those of mixed blood). Jefes also promulgated official announcements, oversaw the creation of schools and courts, tallied censuses, safeguarded public morality, presided at public events, and kept the governor abreast of all developments. Job requirements such as functional literacy and a command of Spanish excluded 95 percent of the population. Actual performance ranged from even-handed to rankly political. The jefe of this novella tends to fluctuate between the two extremes but finds himself obliged to act fairly when under the public gaze. Revolutionary chief Venustiano Carranza abolished the office in 1915 as part of his dismantling of the Porfirian apparatus.

35. It is difficult to assign a simple conversion value to the sum of twenty pesos. The way that we live now is so utterly different that one finds few items for accurate comparison of costs. But for our purposes we might suppose a ratio of 1:100 when converting to modern currency. Suffice to say that twenty pesos constituted a huge amount of money for a rural gardener.

36. *Pipián* is a delicious sauce made from chiles and spices and thickened with ground pumpkin seeds. It is a common food for special events throughout Mexico and Central America.

37. A *chachalaca* bird (genus *Ortalis*, with numerous species) is a form of wild chicken famous for being noisy. López Portillo's confession regarding the pointlessness of shooting these birds exposes one of the peculiarities of late-nineteenth-century western culture, namely, its quest for alternate measures of masculinity. Killing animals for the heck of it usually helped.

38. López Portillo's positivist roots show in this incredible passage. His reflections on the future of Mexico's rural poor resemble what some therapists say of alcoholics: that they will only pull out of their problems when they hit

rock bottom. Apparently for López Portillo the conditions of walking around half-naked, living on roasted pumpkin, and enduring sexual violation at the hands of property owners did not qualify as such.

39. This second and equally incredible remark might be taken as irony, except that López Portillo is dead serious. He seems not to have perceived that the experiments in question involved episodes of fasting among relatively healthy, well-fed humans and in fact said little to nothing about the long-term effects of nutritional deficiency.

40. That is, mounted workers or cowboys.

41. In the language of the Mexican *charrería*, *caracolear*, or to move in a circle resembling the spiral of a snail's shell.

42. Tule, or tulle, is a thin, fine fiber netting often used in petticoats and wedding gowns. In this instance the author presumably refers to cushions covered in tulle.

43. This is an interesting play of words, as "amo" means both "love" and "master," the latter referring to matters of employment or property. Petra is taunting Don Santos to control the wayward Nieves.

44. The Castilian or Damask rose comes in a variety of colors, ranging from blood red to baby pink.

45. The clear suggestion here is that Don Santos allows his workers to rough up the unwanted Juan.

46. One can only wonder how much López Portillo actually knew of what he calls "oriental songs," but perhaps the comment reflects his travels in the Middle East.

47. As this interesting passage reveals, much of the business of justice involved saving face. In this regard, the jefe político manages to get the better of Don Santos.

48. The fact that the narrator's family has a house directly on the plaza tags family members as wealthy citizens of the town, a reliable status symbol in the Mexico of years gone by.

49. *Bagazo* refers to the remains of any crop that has been crushed for its juices, notably sugar cane. The question of what to do with bagazo has always been a problem. Even as late as revolutionary Cuba, people have experimented with uses—fertilizer, animal fodder, even briquettes—but usually it gets thrown away. In this instance, the term *tuba* refers to *bagazo*, but in other usages is a type of liquor made from coconut or palm. It is believed to have originated in the Philippines and would thus have become known in Jalisco via Spain's trade with Asia.

50. [López Portillo's note:] "The recent visit by the Swiss explorer Lumholtz to the Jalisco region inhabited by the Huicholes has clarified this point. The

industry is pre-Hispanic. The Huicholes still extract alcohol using the same system employed earlier in Tequila, the alcohol being contained in the saccharine base of a plant called *sotol*, quite similar to mezcal." Matías de la Mota Padilla (Guadalajara, 1688–1776) was a jurist by training and profession. Among other accomplishments, he founded the University of Guadalajara in 1792. He is remembered today as the author of *Historia de la Nueva Galicia*, completed in 1742 and providing laudatory accounts of the region's Spanish settlers. López Portillo probably knew of the *Historia* from its first printing in Mexico in 1871. *Tepachi*, or *tepache*, refers in this instance to a fermented beverage made from fruit peals and brown sugar. In Veracruz at roughly this same time, the term referred to a mixture of aguardiente, water, sugar, and lime (think daquiris). *Tesgüino* is a rustic corn beer much favored by the Tarahumara peoples of the northwest Sierra Madres but certainly known in other parts of western Mexico.

51. Paris hosted five expositions, or world's fairs, between 1855 and 1937. The novel's 1887 publication date rules out reference to the most famous of these, the 1889 Exposition Universelle, which gave us the Eiffel Tower and in which Jalisco cigar manufacturer Heraclio Farías did indeed win an international prize for his invention, a cigar-rolling machine.

52. Even today the juice from the agave heart, however obtained, is still called *aguamiel*, or "honey water."

53. The term "must" (or in Spanish, "*mosto*") comes from viticulture and originally refers to the juice extracted from pressed grapes.

54. [López Portillo's note:] "In the foregoing lines I have described the old way of working the mezcal. Modern times have seen considerable improvements in the process. Except for the oven used to *tatemar*, which remains the same, many factories have done away with the *tahona*, the vats, and the ladles, all of which formed the basis of the old method."

55. By the time this novella was published, the term "Your Mercy" *(su merced)* was becoming an antiquated relic of the colonial era. López Portillo invokes it here and elsewhere in the narrative to indicate how backward and isolated rural Jalisco really was.

56. An *ayuntamiento* was and is a city council.

57. Progress and criminality rose together in the Porfiriato. At the time of López Portillo's writing, the prison was a new institution in Mexico, the oldest being Mexico City's Belem Prison, based on the ideas of Jeremy Benthem (1748–1832) and opened in 1886. Legumberri Prison opened fourteen years later and became something of a Porfirian Supermax. Today it serves as the National Archives.

58. The *pronunciamiento*, or pronouncement, was a document making known the aims of a group of individuals who had taken up arms against the

government. It was circulated to gain support among the people and supposedly separated those who pronounced from common criminals. López Portillo obviously has his doubts about the distinction.

59. The term *desgraciado* was a catch-all term for anyone considered immoral, villainous, or generally worthless.

60. By referring to the men as *guardias*, López Portillo distinguishes them from trained, professional soldiers. They were essentially a posse.

61. This is López Portillo's roundabout way of saying that the "captain" was accustomed to the sudden surprise attacks that were an essential of guerrilla warfare.

62. Camotes are a type of sweet potato, often perceived as poor folks' food. The "stores" in question were called *tendejones*, small establishments selling all sorts of tools, dry goods, foodstuffs, and above all alcohol. Throughout the entirety of rural Mexico it was common for men to gather at the tendejones, converse, and share a few drinks. As might be imagined, tendejones were also the scenes of quite a few fights.

63. The narrator refers to Miguel Hidalgo y Costilla (1753–1811), the priest whose anarchic rebellion in Mexico's central mining district eventually led to independence. For a Mexican blue blood of conservative inclinations, López Portillo offers an extraordinarily forgiving view of Hidalgo, some indicator of the way that the rebel's image had been whitewashed and coopted by ruling elites.

64. Obviously, "shotted" is not a word. To capture Juan's rural dialect, López Portillo has him say "*ajusilado*" instead of "*fusilado*," that is, "shot." Dialect is rare in his writings and clearly not his forte.

65. A toned-down version of Spanish profanity, in which the word *madre*, or "mother," figures in countless permutations.

66. An odd comment, given the fact that her face was almost entirely covered.

67. As stated in the introduction, López Portillo's account of Tequila resistance is highly exaggerated. The real Lozada entered the town virtually unopposed.

68. The *ocote*, or *Pinus montezumae*, is a thickly resinous pine tree found throughout much of Mesoamerica. Its core burns easily, which made it popular for torches. The strong, sweet aromas also rendered it useful in religious ceremonies of the indigenous peoples.

69. The term *camino real* applied to any of the main roads of colonial Mexico. Caminos reales typically became the basis for later highways. The term is still used for certain stretches of roadway in places like Texas and California, a nod to those states' colonial Spanish heritage.

The Bracelet

1. San Lorenzo, or Saint Lawrence (225–258) was a Spanish-born convert to Christianity. His hagiography tells that he was martyred by being roasted alive on a hot grill. According to the time-honored legend, he told his torturers to turn him over because he was already done on one side.

2. Then as now, one of the key attractions to the city of Veracruz is the fortification of San Juan de Ulúa that guards the harbor. Constructed in the 1530s as a protection against pirates, it became a hellish prison under Porfirio Díaz and now serves as one of the state's principal tourist attractions.

3. The nickname of Veracruz is the Four-Times Heroic City. But one of those occasions—the US occupation of 1914—had yet to occur by the time of López Portillo's writing.

4. Mexico's first rail line, running from Mexico City to Veracruz, was built by entrepreneur Antonio Escandón. He secured rights to the enterprise in 1857, but the line did not come into operation until 1873. By the time that López Portillo wrote, hundreds of miles of other lines had appeared in the country. Almost all were foreign-financed and constructed. Escandón's original line continued in service.

5. López Portillo presumably has Guadalajara in mind, as this destination would have been his likely path after continuing on from Mexico City.

6. Actually, the time necessary for the journey in question would have been somewhere on the order of three days: one for the boat journey from Havana to Veracruz, one to rest up in the port, and one more for the train ride to Mexico City.

Bibliography

Alfaro, Alfonso. "El tequila y sus signos: Elogio del hidalgo campirano." In *El Tequila: Arte tradicional de México*, edited by Alberto Ruy Sánchéz Lacy and Margarita de Orellana, 10–15. 3rd ed. Mexico City: Artes de México, 2008.

Binhammer, Katherine. *Downward Mobility: The Form of Capital and the Sentimental Novel*. Baltimore: Johns Hopkins University Press, 2020.

Botello, Salvador, ed. *El antiguo método de elaboración del vino mexcal de Tequila descrito en la novela Nieves del siglo XIX por José López Portillo y Rojas*. Illustrations by Ignacio Gómez Arriola. Guadalajara: Taller de Gráfica de Comala, 2022.

Brittsen, Zachary. *Popular Politics and Rebellion in Mexico: Manuel Lozada and La Reforma, 1855–1876*. Nashville: Vanderbilt University Press, 2015.

Brushwood, John S. *Mexico and Its Novel: A Nation's Search for Identity*. Austin: University of Texas Press, 1966.

Chang-Rodríguez, Raquel, and Malva E. Filer. *Voces de Hispanoamérica: Antología literaria*. 3rd ed. Boston: Heinl & Heinl Publishers, 1996.

Curley, Robert. *Citizens and Believers: Religion and Politics in Revolutionary Jalisco, 1900–1930*. Albuquerque: University of New Mexico Press, 2018.

Dabove, Juan Pablo. *Nightmares of the Lettered City: Banditry and Literature in Latin America, 1816–1929*. Pittsburgh: University of Pittsburgh Press, 2007.

Delpar, Helen. *The Enormous Vogue of Things Mexican: Cultural Relations between the United States and Mexico, 1920–1935*. Tuscaloosa: University of Alabama Press, 1992.

Foster, George M. "Peasant Society and the Image of Limited Good." *American Anthropologist* 67(2) (1965): 293–315.

González Peña, Carlos. *History of Mexican Literature*. Translated by Gusta Barfield Nance and Florene Johnson Dunstan. Dallas: Southern Methodist University Press, 1968, orig. 1943.

Grass, Roland. *José López Portillo y Rojas: A Novelist of Social Reform in Mexico to the Revolution of 1910.* Macomb, IL: Western Illinois University, 1970.

Guerra, François-Xavier. *México del antiuo régimen a la revolución.* Translated by Sergio Fernández Bravo. Mexico City: Fondo de Cultura Económica, 2010. Originally published in 1985.

Herrera, Modesto L. "Voto particular del Diputado Modesto L. Herrera, miembro de la Primera Sección instructora del Gran Jurado, en la acusación hecho al Señor José López Portillo y Rojas." Nettie Lee Benson Latin American Collection, University of Texas at Austin.

"A History of the World's Oldest Tequila Brand." Cuervo.com.

Jáurregui, Jesús. "Mexcaltitán-Aztlán: Un nuevo mito." *Arqueología mexicana* 12 (67) (2004): 56–61.

Katz, Friedrich. *The Life and Times of Pancho Villa.* Stanford: Stanford University Press, 1998.

Langford, Walter M. *The Mexican Novel Comes of Age.* Notre Dame: University of Notre Dame Press, 1971.

López Portillo y Rojas, José. *Francisco I. Madero.* Mexico City: SA Coyocán, 1976. Extracted and reprinted from *Elevación y caída de Porfirio Díaz.* Mexico City: Libería Española, 1921.

———. *Obras de D. J. López Portillo y Rojas*, 4 vols. Mexico City: V. Agüeros, 1898–1909.

MacGregor, Josefina. "José López Portillo y Rojas." In *Cancilleres de México: 1910–1988.* 99–121. Mexico City: Secretaría de Relaciones Exteriores, 1992.

Martín-Flores, Mario. "Nineteenth-Century Prose Fiction." In *Mexican Literature: A History*, edited with translations by David William Foster, 112–37. Austin: University of Texas Press, 1994.

Meyer, Michael C. *Huerta: A Political Portrait.* Lincoln: University of Nebraska Press, 1972.

Morris, Nathaniel. *Soldiers, Saints, and Shamans: Indigenous Communities and the Revolutionary State in Mexico's Gran Nayar, 1910–1940.* Tucson: University of Arizona Press, 2020.

Muriá, José María. *Breve historia de Jalisco.* Prologue by Miguel León-Portillo. Guadalajara: Secretaría de Educación Pública, 1988.

———. "Momentos del tequila: El agave histórico." In *El Tequila: Arte tradicional de México*, edited by Alberto Ruy Sánchéz Lacy and Margarita de Orellana, 16–25. 3rd ed. Mexico City: Artes de México, 2008.

Orellana, Margarita de. "Microhistoria del tequila: El caso Cuervo." In *El Tequila: Arte tradicional de México*, edited by Alberto Ruy Sánchéz Lacy and Margarita de Orellana, 28–35. 3rd ed. Mexico City: Artes de México, 2008.

Parkes, Henry Bamford. *A History of Mexico.* New York: Houghton Mifflin, 1969. Originally published in 1938.

Poe, Edgar Allen. *The Complete Tales & Poems of Edgar Allen Poe.* Introduction by Wilbur C. Scott. New York: Castle Books, 2002. Originally published in 1985.

Rama, Ángel. *La ciudad letrada.* Hanover, NH: Ediciones del Norte, 1984.

Reyes, Juan José. *Cuestión de suerte.* Mexico City: Clío, 1997.

Rigdon, Susan M. *The Culture Facade: Art, Science, and Politics in the Work of Oscar Lewis.* Urbana: University of Illinois Press, 1988.

Sánchez y Lacy, Alberto Ruy, and Margarita de Orellano, eds. *El tequila: Arte tradicional de México.* México: Artes de México, 2008. Originally published in 1995.

Sloan, Kathryn A. *Runaway Daughters: Seduction, Elopement, and Honor in Nineteenth-Century Mexico.* Albuquerque: University of New Mexico Press, 2008.

Sommer, Doris. *Foundational Fictions: The National Romances of Latin America.* Berkeley: University of California Press, 1991.

Stephens, Michele McArdle. *In the Lands of Fire and Sun: Resistance and Accommodation in the Huichol Sierra, 1723–1930.* Lincoln: University of Nebraska Press, 2018.

Valenzuela-Zapata, Ana G., and Gary Paul Nabham. *¡Tequila! A Natural and Cultural History.* Tucson: University of Arizona Press, 2003.

Vigil, José. "La Reforma." In *México a través de los siglos,* edited by Vicente Riva Palacio, vol. 9. Mexico City: Editorial Cumbre, 1962. Originally published in 1884.